ISBN 978-0-483-99002-9
PIBN 10797416

WELCOME:

A BOOK OF

HYMNS, SONGS AND LESSONS.

FOR THE

CHILDREN OF THE NEW CHURCH.

THIRD EDITION.

THE NEW CHURCH BOARD OF PUBLICATION:
NEW YORK: 20 COOPER UNION;
BOSTON: MASS. NEW CHURCH UNION;
CHICAGO: NEW CHURCH BOOKSTORE;
PHILADA: J. B. LIPPINCOTT & CO.
1876.

PREFACE.

THIS little book is designed to meet the wants felt in many Sunday-schools of having, instead of an accumulation of Song Books, Catechisms, Question Books, etc., a single inexpensive volume which shall contain a variety of materials needed in the *general* exercises of the school. It is hoped that it will also, as a practical manual and guide, afford assistance to those who are organizing new schools, and especially in the formation and conduct of mission-schools. Many who would like to undertake such work hesitate for want of experience and for not knowing "how to begin." We hope that they will find here, in some measure, the direction and assistance they need.

We trust, too, that the "Welcome" will find its way into many homes where few or no privileges of public worship and religious instruction are enjoyed, and there be a messenger of love and truth from the "Holy city, which descends out of Heaven from God."

It will be understood, of course, that this book is not intended to cover *all*, but only some general needs of the school. Special books of instruction should be provided for the several classes in the grades of their respective advancement, such as Lessons on the Lord's Prayer, on the Ten Commandments, and other Biblical and doctrinal text-books.

For the musical part of the "Welcome" we are very largely indebted to Mr. George F. Root, by whom a great number of the tunes are composed, and to his fellow-compilers of the beautiful series of "Song-Birds" and the "Chapel Gems." Our thanks are also due to the authors and proprietors of the pieces on pages 53, 62, 66, 68, and 72, for their kind permission to use them in this work.

The Catechism is that known, and already, to some extent, in use in this country, as the "Child's First Catechism"—prepared by the New Church Conference in England.

We call our little book the "Welcome," because we hope that, like a good angel standing at the gate of the New Jerusalem, it may give a friendly greeting and happy reception to many little children, who, by its means, shall learn to love and do the commandments of God, and thus "enter in, through the gates, into the city."

F. S.

Glendale, O., Sept., 1868.

Note—In mentioning certain books of instruction in the "Suggestions," page 2, Second Part, it is not intended to recommend these books especially in preference to others, but only to indicate the kind of instruction suitable for this part of the school exercises. To the books there mentioned we may add the following, which have lately appeared at the Publishing House,—*The Child's True Christian Religion; A Catechism on the Lord's Prayer*, by the Rev. Mr. Perry; *My Little Guide*, a book of verses and questions for little children.

TABLE OF CONTENTS.

THE WELCOME.

Hosanna.

"And the multitudes that went before, and that followed, cried. saying. Hosanna to the Son of David: blessed is He that cometh in the name of the Lord: Hosanna in the highest!"

Ho - san - na, Ho - san - na, Ho - san - - -

na; Bless - ed is He, Bless - ed, bless - ed is

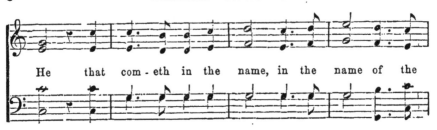

He　　that　com - eth　in　the　name,　in　the　name　of　the

Lord.　Ho - san - - - na,　　Ho - san - - - na,　　Ho -

san................na,　　Ho - san - na　in　the　high-est,　　Ho -

san - na　in　the　high-est,　　in　the　high - - est.

MODERATO

1. Chil-dren of Je - ru - sa - lem, Place the roy - al di - a - dem
2. Come, let ev - 'ry heart and tongue, Join and swell the grate-ful song:
3. Par - ents, Teachers, old and young, All u - nite and swell the song;

On the Sav-ior's head, and raise Sa - cred an-thems to His praise.
Sweet - er, high - er, let us sing, Loud Ho - san - nas to our King.
High - er, and yet high - er rise, Let the cho - rus reach the skies.

Join, with heart and voice, to sing Loud Ho - san - nas to our King:

Join, with heart and voice, to sing Loud Ho - san - nas to our King.

Grant Thy Blessing. (Opening.)

1. Ho - ly   Fa - ther, grant thy bless - ing, To   us   chil - dren
2. Bless the   teach - ers thou hast giv - en, And our   pas - tor,

of thy care; Glad we meet thy name con - fess - ing, In   thy
whom we love; Guide us till we   all, in hea - ven, Meet with-

ho - ly house of prayer. May the les - sons we are learn - ing,
in thy courts a - bove. There we'll join the heaven-ly cho - rus,

From thy   ho - ly Word to - day; Help our   fee - ble
With the   dear ones gone be - fore; Hail the Prince of

feet while turn - ing   To the straight and nar - row way.
Peace most glo - rious, Love and serve thee   ev - er - more.

Our Father, Teach Us. (OPENING.)

G. F. R.

1. Our   Fa - ther, teach   us   how   to   pray,   As
2. For - give   the   sins   that   we   have wrought, And
3. As   thou   hast loved   us, may we   love   Each

in thine house we   meet; How   wor - thi - ly our
give us grace to   shun Each wick - ed - ness of
oth - er   day by   day,   Till with thine an - gel

gifts   to   lay   Be - fore   thy   mer - cy   seat.
deed   and thought That hands and hearts have done.
band   a - bove   We   praise in - stead   of   pray.

Wo Come to Thy Temple. (OPENING.)   H. W. J.

1. We come to Thy tem - ple, O Sa - vior of love,
2. Oh! grant us Thy bless - ings of wis - dom and truth,

To ask of the high - way that lead - eth a - bove,
And be Thou our Strength in the morn - ing of youth;

To list to Thy pre - cepts— to learn of Thy will,
That we from Thy ser - vice may nev - er de - part,

That all Thy com - mand - ments our lives may ful - fil.
But toil on with cour - age and new - ness of heart.

We Praise Thee. (Opening or Closing.)

G. F. R. 13

1. We praise Thee—we bless Thee, our Fath - er, and Friend,
2. We thank Thee for bless - ings re - ceived eve - ry day—
3. Pro - tect us— de - fend us from sin and from harm,

O let our de - vo - tions be - fore Thee as - cend;
For which Thou hast taught us un - ceas - ing to pray;
As the shep - herd doth gath - er the lambs with his arm;

In youth and in child - hood, to - geth - er we come,
But O, for the treas - ures Thy Word hath in store,
O nour - ish and strength - en our souls now in youth,

To pray that Thy will in our hearts may be done.
Thy name, O, our Fath - er we bless and a - dore
With Thy love and Thy wis - dom,—Thy good - ness and truth.

Draw Nigh to Us.

1. Draw nigh to us, our Fath - er, By draw-ing us to thee,
2. We hail Thee throned in glo - ry—'Mid heaven's angelic throng,

And may we here to - geth - er, Thy wondrous glo - ry see,
Who cast their crowns be - fore Thee With ev - er - last - ing song.

The sun it shin-eth ev - er, Though clouds are o'er 'its light,
Thy good-ness yet re - joi - ces Love's humblest note to hear,

Thy love would cheer us ev - er If sin dimm'd not our sight.
May then our fee-blest voi - ces At - tract Thy gracious ear.

REVERENTIALLY

1. Je - sus, gent - lest   Sa - vior;   God   of   might and pow'r.
2. Out   be -yond   the   shin - ing   Of   the   far - thest star;
3. Je - sus, gent - lest   Sa - vior;   Thou   art   in   us   now.

Make   Thy   ho - ly   dwell - ing   In   us   at   this hour.
Thou   art   ev - er   stretch - ing,   In - fi - nite - ly   far—
Fill   us   full   of   good - ness,   'Till   our hearts o'er flow.

Na - ture   can - not   hold   thee,   Heav'n is   all   too strait
Yet   the   hearts of   chil - dren,   Hold what worlds can - not—
Pray   the   pray'r with - in   us,   That   to heav'n shall rise.

For   thine   end - less   glo - ry,   And   thy   roy - al   state.
And   the   God   of   won - ders   Loves the   low - ly   spot.
Sing   the   song that - an - gels,   Sing   a - bove   the skies.

Happy Hearts Children Bring.

G. F. R.

MODERATO.

1. Hap - py hearts chil - dren bring, Now to God the of - fer - ing;
2. Thank - ful hearts chil - dren bring, As a trib - ute to their King;
3. Lov - ing hearts chil - dren bring, An - gels bear the of - fer - ing,

Sing his praise, learn his ways On this best, this best of days.
God is near, Fa - ther hear, And ac - cept my hum - ble pray'r.
To the Lamb, bless - ed name, An - gels catch the joy - ful strain.

God is love, then let us sing Prais - es to our Sav - ior King.
God is love, and chil-dren raise Thank-ful hearts in songs of praise.
God is love, and an - gels join Our glad cho - rus round the throne.

Savior, We, thy Children, Gather.

B. R. H.

MODERATO.

1. Sav - ior, we, thy chil-dren, gath-er In thy bless-ed courts to - day;
2. Thou wilt trace the path be - fore us, We shall walk and nev - er stray
3. We would clasp thine hand for-ev - er, In the dark-ness as the day,

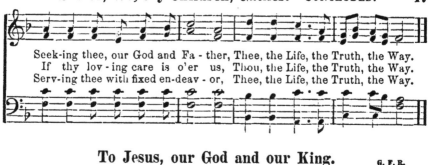

Seek-ing thee, our God and Fa - ther, Thee, the Life, the Truth, the Way.
If thy lov - ing care is o'er us, Thou, the Life, the Truth, the Way.
Serv-ing thee with fixed en-deav - or, Thee, the Life, the Truth, the Way.

To Jesus, our God and our King.

G. F. R.

MODERATO.

1. To Je - sus, our God and our King, Our
2. His good - ness is o - ver us all, His
3. O then let us all love him more, And

voi - ces we'll joy - ful - ly raise; And glad - ly his
lov - ing care keeps us from harm; And though we are
try to o - bey his com-mands; That we on the

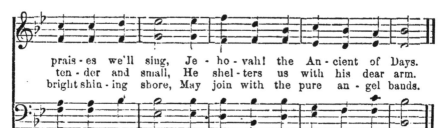

prais - es we'll sing, Je - ho - vah! the An - cient of Days.
ten - der and small, He shel - ters us with his dear arm.
bright shin - ing shore, May join with the pure an - gel bands.

We come in Childhood's Joyfulness.

ANDANTINO

1. We come in child - hood's joy - ful - ness, We
   We of - fer up, O God! our hearts, In
2. We come not as the might - y come; Not
   But as the pure in heart should bend; Seek
3. To Thee thou Lord of life and light, A -
   We bend the knee we lift the heart, And

come, as chil - dren, free!
trust - ing love to Thee.
as the proud we bow;
we thine al - tars now.
mid the an - gel throng,
swell the ho - ly song.

Well may we bend in
"For - bid them not," the
How blest the chil - dren

sol - emn joy, At thy bright courts a - bove;
Sav - ior said; But let them come to me;
of the Lord Who wait a - round His throne,

RITARD

Well may the grate-ful child re-joice, In such a Fa-ther's love.
Oh Sav - ior dear we hear Thy call, We come, we come to Thee.
How sweet to tread the path that leads To yon - der heavenly home,

MODERATE.

1. To Thee, O God, we of - fer Our joy - ful songs of praise;
2. Guard Thou our lives, we pray thee, From sin and er - ror's ways;

To Thee, the boun-teous Giv - er, And Guard-ian of our days:
Show us the path of du - ty, And guide thro' fu - ture days:

A - gain we meet to thank Thee, To raise our ev'n-ing pray'r;
May youth and age so serve Thee, Thou God of watch-ful love;

Our hearts are fill'd with glad - ness For Thy most ten - der care.
That we when life is end - ed, May dwell with Thee a - bove.

"To God, the Father, Spirit, Son."

F. S.

1. To God, the Fa - ther, Spir - it, Son, In soul and mind and
Be glo - ry, praise and ser - vice given, By all on earth and
2. In child-hood's bliss - ful days de - scend, In - spire us for our
And when our out-ward na - ture dies, Own us thy chil - dren

per - son one, } Je - sus, our Lord, we praise in thee
all in heav'n: }
be - ing's end; } To thee our morn - ing song of praise,
in the skies: }

The ev - er bless - ed Trin - i - ty; And while be - fore thy
To thee our ev'n - ing pray'r we raise; Thy glo - ry sup-pliant

throne we fall, We own thee God and Lord of all.
we a - dore For - ev - er and for ev - er - more.

W. H. MONK.

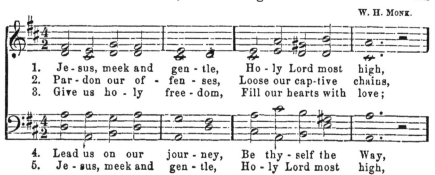

1. Je - sus, meek and gen - tle, Ho - ly Lord most high,
2. Par - don our of - fen - ses, Loose our cap-tive chains,
3. Give us ho - ly free - dom, Fill our hearts with love;

4. Lead us on our jour - ney, Be thy - self the Way,
5. Je - sus, meek and gen - tle, Ho - ly Lord most high,

Pity - ing, lov - ing Sav - ior, Hear thy chil - dren's cry.
Break down ev - 'ry i - dol Which our soul de - tains.
Draw us, Ho - ly Je - sus, To the realms a - bove.

Thro' ter - res - trial dark - ness, To ce - les - tial day.
Pity - ing, lov - ing Sav - ior, (*omit*.................................)

Last verse—last line.

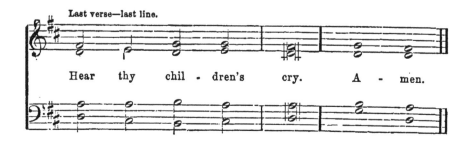

Hear thy chil - dren's cry. A - men.

Let us, with a Gladsome Mind.

G. F. R.

MODERATO.

1. Let us, with a glad-some mind, Praise the Lord, for He is kind;
2. All things round us He has made, All things liv-ing He does feed;
3. All who love Him He will bless With e - ter - nal joy and peace;
4. Let us, then, with gladsome mind, Praise the Lord, for He is kind;

For His mer-cies shall en - dure, Ev - er faith-ful, ev - er sure.
For His mer-cies shall en - dure, Ev - er faith-ful, ev - er sure
For His mer-cies shall en - dure, Ev - er faith-ful, ev - er sure.
For His mer-cies shall en - dure, Ev - er faith-ful, ev - er sure.

Now to Jesus Christ the Glory.

G. F. R.

MODERATO.

Now to Je-sus Christ the glo - ry And do - min-ion shall be given;

He is Al - pha and O - me - ga, First and last in earth and heaven.

G. F. R.

Oh may we Thank-ful be, For the wondrous fa - vor
Of Thy word, Bless-ed Lord, Mak-er, King and (*omit*) Sav - ior.

May Thy Love.—(Closing.)

1. May Thy love, O God our Sav - ior, In - to all our
2. Thou our Fa - ther—we a - dore Thee, Thou the Fa - ther

hearts de - scend; May Thy wis - dom lead and guide us,
in the Son; God and Fa - ther, Son and Sav - ior,

And from ev - 'ry ill de - fend.
In Thy glo - rious per - son One.

"Prince of Glory."—Closing. B. R. H.

Bless - ed Je - sus, Prince of Glo - ry, Thee we wor - ship,

thee a - dore; We are thine, for thou hast saved us,

Keep us thine for - ev - er - more, Keep us thine,

Keep us thine, Keep us thine for - ev - er - more.

O most mer - ci - ful, Good and boun - ti - ful,

Je - sus, Sav - ior, our God and King!

Thy bless - ing send us, From ill de - fend us;

Glo - ry be thine, for - ev - er we sing!

END OF PART FIRST.

PART II.

THE LIFE OF OUR LORD UPON EARTH.

When His Salvation Bringing.

F. 8

1. When his sal - va - tion bring - ing, To Zi - on Je - sus came;
2. And since the Lord re - tain - eth His love for chil - dren still,
3. For should we fail pro - claim - ing Our great Re - deem - er's praise,

The chil - dren all stood sing - ing Ho - san - na to his name;
Tho' now as King he reign - eth On Zi - on's heav'n - ly hill,
The stones, our si - lence sham - ing, Would their Ho - san - na raise;

Nor did their zeal of - fend him, But, as he went a - long,
We'll flock a - round his ban - ner, Who sits up - on the throne;
Then flock a - round his ban - ner, Who sits up - on the throne;

26

He   let them still at - tend Him, And smiled to hear their song;
And   shout a - loud "Ho - san - na To   Da - vid's roy - al   Son;"
And   cry to Him, "Ho - san - na," Who reign-eth God a - lone;

He   let them still at - tend Him, And smiled to hear their song
And   shout a - loud "Ho - san - na To   Da - vid's roy - al   Son."
And   cry to Him, "Ho - san - na," Who reign-eth God a - lone.

Long Ago.

B. R. H.

MODERATO

1. Long a - go, when lit - tle chil-dren Came, the lov-ing Lord to see,
2. Lit - tle chil-dren, now to Je - sus Come, with lov-ing, trusting heart;
3. While He on the earth was liv-ing, If He saw one meek and mild,
4. Tho' He died, He lives in Heav-en, And His care en - folds us still;

Jesus bless'd them, Jesus loved them, Just such lit-tle ones as we.
From the world a - bove He sees us, He will bless us ere we part.
Gen-tle, truth-ful, and for - giv-ing, Well He lov'd that lit - tle child.
To us all His love is giv - en When we do His ho - ly will.

Little Children in the Temple.

B. R. H.

ALLEGRETTO.

1. See the Sa - vior in the tem - ple, Giv - ing sight to
2. Oh how sweet the glad ho - san - nas, Peal - ing from that
3. Still the Lord is in His Tem - ple, In the pow - er

blind - ed eyes; Giv - ing life to dy - ing mor - tals,
hap - py throng; Some would hush the child - ish strain, but
of His Word; Come, with grat - i - tude, a - dor - ing,

REFRAIN

Hark, the songs of chil - dren rise. Sing lit - tle chil - dren
Well He loves the in - fant song. Sing &c.
Come, ye chil - dren, praise the Lord. Sing &c.

sing, Hail your Sa - vior King, While for all His

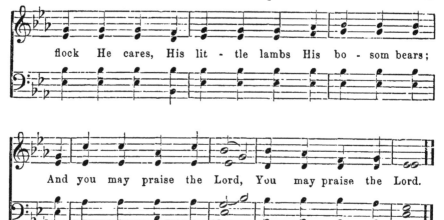

flock He cares, His lit - tle lambs His bo - som bears;

And you may praise the Lord, You may praise the Lord.

Oh Yes, the Lord loved Children.

D. S. A.

MODERATO

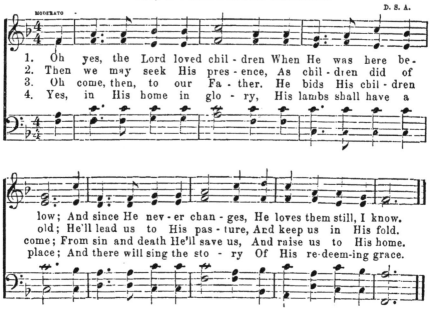

1. Oh yes, the Lord loved chil - dren When He was here be -
2. Then we may seek His pres - ence, As chil - dren did of
3. Oh come, then, to our Fa - ther. He bids His chil - dren
4. Yes, in His home in glo - ry, His lambs shall have a

low; And since He nev - er chan - ges, He loves them still, I know.
old; He'll lead us to His pas - ture, And keep us in His fold.
come; From sin and death He'll save us, And raise us to His home.
place; And there will sing the sto - ry Of His re-deem-ing grace.

Who is He?

B. R. H.

The Teacher's part *may* be uttered in the speech voice.

MODERATO

1. *T.* Who is He in yon - der stall, At whose
2. " Who is He in yon - der cot, Bend - ing
3. " Who is He who stands and weeps At the
4. " Who is He in deep dis - tress, Fast - ing

5. " Lo at mid - night who is He, Prays in
6. " Who is He in Cal - v'ry's throes, Asks for
7. " Who is He that from the grave Comes to
8. " Who is He that on yon Throne, Rules the

CHORUS.

feet the shep - herds fall? 'Tis the Lord, O, won - drous
to His toil - some lot? 'Tis the Lord, &c.
grave where Laz - 'rus sleeps?
in the wil - der - ness?

dark Geth - sem - a - ne?
bless - ings on His foes?
heal, and help and save?
world of light a - lone?

sto - ry, 'Tis the Lord, The King of Glo - ry, At His

feet we hum - bly fall, Crown Him, Crown Him, Lord of all.

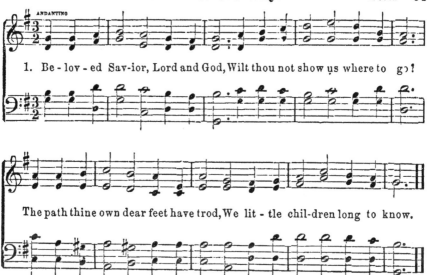

1. Be - lov - ed Sav-ior, Lord and God, Wilt thou not show us where to go?

The path thine own dear feet have trod, We lit - tle chil-dren long to know.

2. Lead us where flow the waters clear,
Of Jordan's consecrating tide;
Thy spirit's voice, Oh, let us hear,
While waiting with thee at its side.

3. And if our onward way should be,
Thro' temptings in the desert drear,
Where angels came to strengthen thee,
Wilt thou, thy self, to us draw near.

Show us the Way.—SECOND HYMN.

1. As thro' the opening skies, came down
To thee, O Lord, the heavenly dove,
Our youthful trust and service crown;
With sweet assurance of thy love.

2. Among the suffering, poor and weak,
Of every clime and every race,

Thy shining foot-prints we will seek,
Our chosen way to help us trace.

3. So, thro' earth's paths and portals low,   (feet;
Walk thou with us and guide our
Till thro' the pearly gates we go,
To walk with thee the golden street.

PART III.

THANKSGIVING AND PRAYER.

Sweet is the Work.

G. F. R.

1. Sweet is the work, O Lord, Thy glo-rious acts to sing, To praise thy name, and
hear thy word, And grate-ful off r-ings bring.

2. Sweet, at the dawning light.
Thy boundless love to tell;
And when approach the shades of night,
Still on the theme to dwell.

3. Sweet, on this day of rest,
To join in heart and voice
With those who love and serve thee best,
And in thy name rejoice.

Thou art Ever Present.

G. F. R.

1. Thou art ev - er pres - ent, Fa-ther, With the chil-dren of thy care Grant-ing bless-ings
2. Help us, O our heav'n-ly Fa-ther, Deep-est grat - i - tude to prove, For thy good-ness

with-out meas-ure, Which we all so free - ly share.
and thy mer-cy, By our words and deeds of love.

3. Grant us strength, O heav'nly Fa-
ther,
Evil thoughts to put away;
Purify our low affections,
Give thy peace from day to day.

4. O, that through the holy teachings,
Which so freely thou dost give,
We may learn to love thy pleasure,
And on earth like angels live.

Thanksgiving.

G. R. H.

JOYFULLY

1. Har-vest fields with gold-en glow, La - den branches, bend-ing low;
2. Lord, we know not how to tell All the thanks our hearts that swell;
3. All we have, Oh, Lord! is Thine, Un - to Thee we all re-sign
4. On each gar - ner and each home, Let Thy crowning bless-ing come;

Crowd-ed gar-ners, clos-ing year, Sing, Thanksgiv-ing - time is here.
Hearts that, full of grate-ful cheer, Sing, Thanksgiv-ing - time is here.
While Thy chil-dren, Fa - ther dear, Sing Thanksgiv-ing - time is here.
While we, nigh the clos-ing year, Sing, Thanksgiv-ing - time is here.

Father, from whose Hand.

G. F. R.

NOT TOO FAST.

1. Fa-ther, from whose hand doth spring Ev-'ry good and per-fect thing,
2. Thou hast placed us here on earth For a high and glo-rious birth;
3. Then, O Fount of ev - 'ry truth, Guard and guide us in our youth;

For the gift of life we raise Songs of grat - i - tude and praise.
And the pre-cious boon hast given To exchange this world for heaven.
Cleanse our souls from ev - 'ry stain, Take them pure to Thee a - gain.

Come, O, blessed Savior.

G. F. R.

MODERATO.

1. Come, O, bless-ed Sav - ior, Rule our hearts to - day;
2. Thou wilt walk be - side us, We shall clasp Thine hand;
3. Aid each meek en - deav - or, Shep - herd of our love,

We will seek Thy fa - vor, We will keep Thy way.
Know - ing it will guide us To the Bet - ter Land.
Till we rest for - ev - er In Thy fold a - bove.

Lord, Thy Word Abideth.

G. F. R.

MODERATO.

1. Lord, Thy word a - bid - eth, And our foot - steps guid - eth!
2. When our foes are near us, Then Thy Word doth cheer us,
3. When the storms are o'er us, And dark clouds be - fore us,
4. Who can tell the pleas - ure, Who re - count the treas - ure,

Who its truth be - liev - eth, Light and joy re - ceiv - eth.
Word of con - so - la - tion, Mes - sage of sal - va - tion.
Then its light di - rect - eth, And our way pro - tect - eth.
By Thy Word im - part - ed To the sim - ple heart - ed.

Savior and Friend.

ANDANTINO

1. Rest of the wea-ry, Joy of the sad, Hope of the drea-ry,
2. Pil-low where ly-ing Love rests its head, Peace of the dy-ing,
3. When my feet stum-ble, To thee I'll cry, Crown of the hum-ble,
4. Ev-er con-fess-ing Thee, I will raise Un-to thee bless-ing,

Light of the glad; Home of the stranger, Strength to the end;
Life of the dead: Path of the low-ly, Prize at the end,
Cross of the high; When my steps wan-der, O-ver me bend
Glo-ry and praise: All my en-deav-or World with-out end,

CHORUS

Ref-uge from dan-ger, Sav-ior and Friend. Rest of the wea-ry
Breath of the ho-ly, Sav-ior and Friend Rest, &c.
Tru-er and fond-er, Sav-ior and Friend. Rest, &c.
Thine to be ev-er Sav-ior and Friend. Rest, &c.

Joy of the sad, Hope of the drea-ry, Light of the glad.

Evening Song.

G. F. R.

ANDANTINO.

1. The ev'n-ing dews are fall-ing Up-on the si-lent lawn;
2. The wea-ry bird has fold-ed Her tiu-y wings to rest;
3. O Sav-ior, grant thy bless-iug, When ev'n-ing shad-ows fall;
4. Our hearts, like fra-grant blos-soms, With love's sweet bloom-ing flow'r,

The fra-grant flow'rs are wait-ing For the ros-y light of dawn.
Her lit-tle form. re-pos-ing Ou her soft and down-y nest.
Like gen-tle dews de-scend-ing In sweet si-lence up-on all.
Would wait thy dai-ly bless-ing In the calm sweet ev'n-ing hour.

The Holy Hour.

B. R. H.

ANDANTINO

1. How sweet the ho-ly hour, When at the throne of grace We come in pray'r to
2. O haste my will-ing feet, To join the hap-py throng; Con-fess thy sius, my
3. The gen-tle Shep-herd flies (O wealth of love un-told!) To hear, and help, and
4. O, Shep-herd, Sav-ior, King, Come, make this heart thy throne; Drive out thy foes, thou

bend the knee, And an-gels fill the place, And an-gels fill the place.
trem-bling lips, Or raise the grate-ful song, Or raise the grate-ful song.
heal and bless The hum-blest of his fold, The hum-blest of his fold.
Might-y One, And make me all thine own, And make me all thine own.

Child's Evening Hymn.

J. R. M.

1. Ho - ly Fa-ther, please to hear me, In my lit - tle hymn to-night;
2. So I bend, and ask Thy bless-ing, Ask Thy par - don and Thy love:

And, my Fa-ther, please be near me Thro' the dark, as in the light:
Sin and fol - ly, all con - fess-ing, Hear me, Fa-ther, from a - bove:

Thou art God, and ser-aphs praise Thee, Countless worlds are all Thine own;
Please to hear me, please to hear me, In my lit - tle hymn to - night;

Yet a child who loves, o-beys Thee, Thou wilt hear, tho' weak, a - lone.
And, my Fa - ther, be Thou near me, Thro' the dark, as in the light.

Prayer at Night.

1. Oh, when up-on my lit-tle bed, I shall lay down my weary head,
2. I know I'm ver-y weak and small, But Thou, O God, tak'st care of all;
3. The wrong that I have done, forgive, And teach me more like Thee to live;
4. I thank Thee for my lit-tle bed, My friends, and for my dai-ly bread,

I pray, my God and Sav-ior, keep Thy child in safe-ty while I sleep.
And by Thy sure pro-tec-tion blest, E-ven a child shall safe ly rest.
And should I die be-fore the light, May angels bear me to Thy sight.
And as I live, Thy love to see, I'll spend my time in prais-ing Thee.

Jesus, the very Thought of Thee.

G. F. R.

1. Je-sus, the ver-y thought of Thee With sweetness fills my breast;
2. Nor voice can sing, nor heart can frame, Nor can the mem-'ry find
3. Oh, hope of ev-'ry con-trite heart, Oh, joy of all the meek,
4. But what to those who find? ah! this Nor tongue nor pen can show;

But sweet-er far Thy face to see, And in Thy presence rest.
A sweet-er sound than Thy blest name, O Sav-ior of man-kind
To those who fall how kind Thou art, How good to those who seek.
The love of Je-sus, what it is, None but his loved ones know.

1. We have come, our heav'n-ly Fa-ther, To thy home to
2. Pity-ing Sav-ior, guard and guide us On the path our
3. We are young, for-bid, Great Shep-herd, That thy ten-der
4. We will love thee and a-dore thee, Where thou lead-est

learn of thee; Young and help-less, yet de-sir-ing,
feet must tread; Un-seen pit-falls are be-fore us,
lambs should stray; Help us, Lord, each day and hour,
fol-low still; Trust-ing-ly with swift o-be-dience,

Lambs of thy own flock to be; Bless-ed Je-sus,
Hid-den snares are round us spread: Give us wis-dom,
Anx-ious-ly to watch and pray; Lest in weak-ness,
Yield sub-mis-sion to thy will; Guide us safe-ly

gra-cious Shep-herd, Thy love is our on-ly plea.
save and strength-en, Lest our souls should faint with dread.
we should fal-ter, And in fal-t'ring lose the way.
to that heav-en, There God's love our souls shall fill.

Here, in Thine House.—Chorale.

1. Here, in Thine house, O God, we meet, And lift our grateful hearts to Thee;
2. We thank Thee, Lord, for life and health, For all things good and all things dear;
3. Be with us, Lord, as Thou hast been; On Thee a-lone our hopes shall rest;

Here may our pray'rs, like incense sweet, Our songs of praise accepted be.
For blessings from Thy love's great wealth; And all the mercies of the year.
Be with us, Lord, thro' life, and then Take us to Thee in Heav-en blest.

O give Thanks unto the Lord.—Chant.

G. F. R.

1. O give thanks unto the Lord, for..	he is good:	For his	mer-cy	is for-	ev-er.
3. O give thanks unto the...............	Lord of lords:	For his	mer-cy	is for-	ev-er.
5. To him that by wisdom...............	made the heav'ns:	For his	mer-cy	is for-	ev-er.
7. To him that...........................	made great lights:	For his	mer-cy	is for-	ev-er.
9. The moon and stars to...............	rule by night:	For his	mer-cy	is for-	ev-er.

2. O give thanks unto the..............	God of gods:	For his	mer-cy	is for-	ev-er.
4. To him who alone.........	doeth great wonders:	For his	mer-cy	is for-	ev-er.
6. To him that stretch'd out the earth a-	bove the waters:	For his	mer-cy	is for-	ev-er.
8. The sun to...........................	rule by day:	For his	mer-cy	is for-	ev-er.
10. O give thanks unto the Lord, for....	he is good:	For his	mer-cy	is for-	ev-er.

PART IV.

SACRED SONGS.

Consider the Lilies.

G. F. R.

1. Con - sid - er how the lil - ies grow, They la - bor not nor spin; Not proud-est kings of

earth we know Such gor-geous ves-tures win: If God so clothe the ten-der flow'r, Now

grow-ing, soon to die; May we not trust our Fa-ther's pow'r? Will he not hear our cry?

2. The floating cloud, the deep blue sky,
   The glorious morn, the day;
The falling leaf, the zephyr's sigh,
   The twilight shadows grey:
The bright-winged warblers of the grove,
   The forest's solemn pray'r,
All whisper of our Father's love,
   His tender, watchful care.

3. His love is Love Divine, and far
   Exceeds our highest thought;
His wisdom beams on high, a star
   Is from its radiance wrought:
The Star of Bethlehem appears,
   To light the darkened way
Of millions, once in grief and tears,
   To immortality.

42

God is Love.

G. F. R.

1. When light-ly o'er the mountain rill The twi-light zephyrs move,
2. The bird that trills its evening song So sweet-ly thro' the grove,
3. The rain-bow in the sum-mer sky Al-might-y Pow'r doth prove,
4. The gold-en stars that night-ly gild The firm-a-ment a-bove,

How sweet-ly to the dew-y flow'rs They whisper God is Love.
In gen-tle ca-dence seems to say, I'll sing, for God is Love.
Man looks up-on its va-ried hue, And owns that God is Love.
In si-lent el-o-quence, proclaim The tidings, God is Love.

Little Flow'ret.

B. R. H.

MODERATO.

1. Lit-tle flow-'ret, press thy way Thro' the dark-ness, in-to day;
2. Bee and blos-som, each ful-fills Pur-po-ses our Fa-ther wills;
3. Like the lit-tle flow'r we press On, to hope and hap-pi-ness;

Ev-'ry-thing shall wel-come thee, Warbling bird, and bus-y bee.
Children should not i-dle be; Sav-ior, let us work for Thee.
Ev-er in God's pur-pose true, Do-ing all that we can do.

Little Eyes.

Geo. B. Loomis.

1. Lit - tle eyes, lit - tle eyes, O - pen with the morn - ing light,
2. Lit - tle heart, lit - tle heart, Full of laugh-ter, full of glee,
3. Lit - tle hands, lit - tle hands, Bus - y with the kite or doll,
4. Lit - tle feet, lit - tle feet, Soft your pat - ter, light your load,

Up - ward look, up - ward look, Heav-en's morn is al - ways bright.
Beat with love, beat with love For the Lord who bless - es thee.
Learn ye may, work or play, Dai - ly to do good to all.
Do not stray, keep the way, Walk the straight and nar - row road.

What Little Things Should Do.

M.

1. Lit - tle knees should low - ly bend, At the time of prayer;
2. Lit - tle hands should use - ful - ly In em - ploy - ment move;
3. Lit - tle tongues should speak the truth, With - out fear or halt;

Lit - tle tho'ts to heav'n as - cend, To our Fa - ther there.
Lit - tle feet should cheer - ful - ly Run on works of love.
Lit - tle lips should ne'er be loth To con - fess a fault.

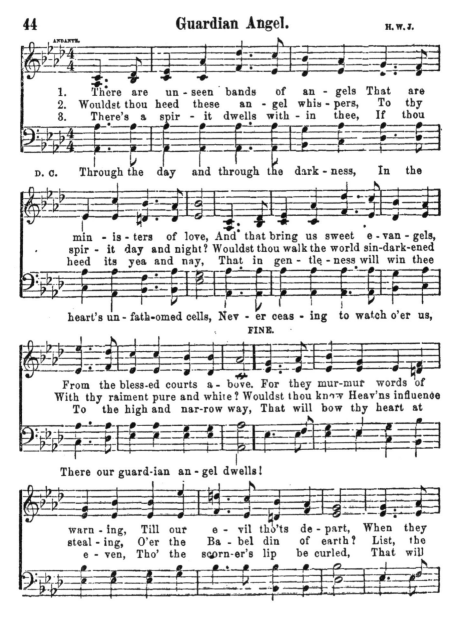

1. There are un-seen bands of an - gels That are
2. Wouldst thou heed these an - gel whis-pers, To thy
3. There's a spir - it dwells with - in thee, If thou

D. C. Through the day and through the dark - ness, In the

min - is - ters of love, And that bring us sweet e - van - gels,
spir - it day and night? Wouldst thou walk the world sin-dark-ened
heed its yea and nay, That in gen - tle - ness will win thee

heart's un - fath-omed cells, Nev - er ceas - ing to watch o'er us,
FINE.

From the bless-ed courts a - bove. For they mur-mur words of
With thy raiment pure and white? Wouldst thou know Heav'ns influence
To the high and nar-row way, That will bow thy heart at

There our guard-ian an - gel dwells!

warn - ing, Till our e - vil tho'ts de - part, When they
steal - ing, O'er the Ba - bel din of earth? List, the
e - ven, Tho' the scorn-er's lip be curled, That will

D. C.

bring the gold - en morn-ing Of sweet peace with-in the heart.
voice-less sweet re - veal - ings Of thy high-er, ho - lier birth.
lead thy heart to Heav - en, To the Sav - ior of the world.

Swiftly Glide the Hours.

G. F. R.

MODERATO.

1. Swift - ly glide the hours a - way, Speed - ing
2. Toil and rest a - like He shares, Bless - es
3. If to - day our lives have been Soil'd by
4. In the dark - ness and the light, Keep us

from us day by day; Leav - ing ev - er,
both our - joys and cares, Makes them all His
thought or deed of sin; Lord, from us the
ev - er in Thy sight; And to Thy dear

as they move, To - kens of our Fa - ther's love.
good - ness prove, Makes them to - kens of His love.
guilt re - move, Fa - ther, par - don in Thy love.
home a - bove, Fa - ther, guide us in Thy love.

"We all might do Good."

G. F. R.

ALLEGRETTO.

1. We all might do good, When we of-ten do ill;
2. We all might do good, In a thou-sand small ways—
3. We all might do good, Wheth-er low-ly or great;

There is al-ways the way, If we have but the will;
In for-bear-ing to flat-ter, Yet yield-ing due praise;
For the deed is not gaged By the purse or es-tate;

Though it be but a word Kind-ly breathed or sup-press'd,
In re-press-ing wrong thought, In re-prov-ing wrong done,
If it be but a cup Of cold wa-ter that's given,

It may ward off some pain, Or give peace to some breast.
And in treat-ing but kind-ly Each heart we have won.
Like "the wid-ow's two mites," It is some-thing for heaven.

1. Who will meet me when I die? Who will lead me
2. When my Sa - vior from on high, Calls my spir - it
3. Who will hush my trem - bling heart? Who will heaven - ly

to the sky? Who will love me in that land? In that heav'n-ly
to the sky, Who will meet me on the strand, Of that heav'n ly
joy im-part? Who will love me in that land? In that heav'n-ly

land, An - gels bright will meet me, An - gels bright, An-gels bright;
land? An - gels bright, &c.
land, An - gels bright, &c.

An - gels bright will meet me, In that heav'n-ly land.

Going Home.

G. F. R.

ANDANTINO.

1. I shall go to Thee my Savior, To my home be-yond the stars,
2. Yet it may be I shall tar-ry Till the noon-tide of life's day,
3. Then I'll go to Thee, my Savior, To my home be-yond the stars,

Where the light is soft-ly gleam-ing Thro' the gates with pearl-y bars;
Or un-til my feet are wea-ry, And my hair is thin and gray;
Where some dear one will be wait-ing By the gate with pearl-y bars;

Where are bands of hap-py child-ren Who have learn'd the ways of truth,
Till the even-ing shadows lengthen, From the glo-ry-tint-ed-west,
Where the wel-come lights are gleaming From the mansions of our rest,

And re-member'd their Cre-a-tor, In the days of ear-ly youth.
And the sil-ver chimes shall call me To the morn-ing of the blest.
And the sil-ver chimes are call-ing To the morn-ing of the blest.

"And they shall be mine, saith the Lord of hosts, in that day when I make up my jewels."

MODERATO.

1. When He com-eth, when He com-eth, To make up his jew-els,
2. He will gath-er, He will gath-er The gems for his king-dom;
3. Lit - tle chil-dren, lit - tle chil-dren, Who love their Re-deem - er,

All his jew - els, pre - cious jew - els, His lov'd and his own.
All the pure ones, all the bright ones, His lov'd and his own.
Are his jew - els, pre - cious jew - els, His lov'd and his own.

CHORUS.

Like the stars of the morn - ing, His bright crown a - dorn - ing,

They shall shine in their beau - ty, Bright gems for his crown

3

The Beacon Light.

G. F. R.

ANDANTINO.

1. We are sail - ing o'er an o - cean, To a far and for - eign shore; And the waves are dash - ing 'round us, And we hear the break - ers roar: But we look a - bove the bil - lows, In the

2. Though the skies are dark a - bove us, And the waves are dash - ing high, Let us look to - ward the bea - con, We shall reach it by and by: 'Tis the light of God's great mer - cy, And He

3. He will keep it ev - er burn - ing, From the light - house of His love; And it al - ways shines the bright - est When the skies are dark a - bove: If we keep our eyes up - on it, And we

dark - ness of the night; And we see the stead - y
holds it up in view, As a guide - star to his
steer our course a - right, We shall reach the har - bor

CHORUS.

gleam - ing Of our change - less bea - con light. O, the
chil - dren, As a guide to me and you. O, &c.
safe - ly, By the bless ed bea - con light. O, &c.

light is flash - ing bright - ly, From a calm and storm - less shore,

Where we hope to cast our an - chor, When our voy - ag - ing is o'er.

We are Watching.—ANNIVERSARY SONG.

G. F. R.

For the opening of the annual meeting of the American New Church S. S. Association.

1. We are watch-ing, we are wait-ing, For the bright pro-phet - ic
2. We are watch-ing, we are wait-ing, For the star that brings the
3. We are watch-ing, we are wait-ing, For the beau-teous King of
4. We are watch-ing, we are wait-ing, For the bright pro-phet - ic

day: When the shad-ows, wea-ry shad-ows, From the world shall
day: When the night of sin shall van - ish, And the shad-ows
day; For the Chief-est of ten thou-sand, For the Light, the
day; When the shad - ows, wea-ry shad-ows, From the world shall

CHORUS.

roll a - way. We are wait-ing for the morn-ing, When the
melt a - way. We are wait - ing &c.
Truth, the Way. We are wait - ing &c.
roll a - way. We are wait-ing &c.

beau-teous day is dawn-ing, We are wait-ing for the morn-ing,

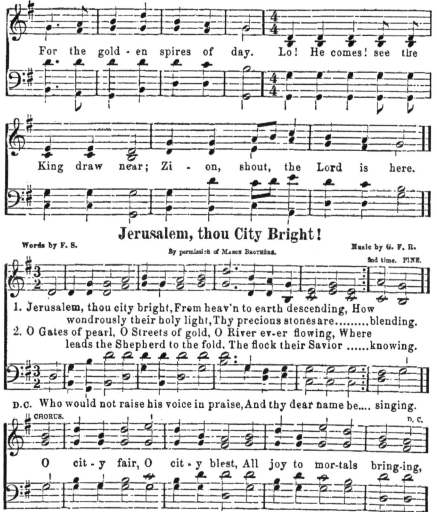

For the gold-en spires of day. Lo! He comes! see the

King draw near; Zi-on, shout, the Lord is here.

Jerusalem, thou City Bright!

Words by F. S.

By permission of Mason Brothers.

Music by G. F. R.

2nd time. FINE.

1. Jerusalem, thou city bright, From heav'n to earth descending, How
wondrously their holy light, Thy precious stones are.........blending.
2. O Gates of pearl, O Streets of gold, O River ev-er flowing, Where
leads the Shepherd to the fold, The flock their Savior ......knowing.

D.C. Who would not raise his voice in praise, And thy dear name be.... singing.

CHORUS.

D. C.

O cit-y fair, O cit-y blest, All joy to mor-tals bring-ing,

3. O Living Stream! O heav'nly Gleam,
New earth and heav n creating;
Shine far and wide, O saving Beam,
Man's wearied soul elating.
   O city fair, &c.

4. Shine, holy Light, within our hearts,
All evil shade dispelling,
That we ne'er from Thy way depart
Which leads to that blest dwelling
   O city fair, &c.

Nothing to Love.

Words by J. R.

Music by G. F. R.

MODERATO.

1. Noth-ing to love! Be si - lent! Mut-ter it not a - gain,—
2. Noth-ing to love! Look up - ward! Look be-yond earth-ly things,
3. There shall we all be gath - ered, Who keep His ho - ly word;

Pro - fan - ing the God who made you— Scorn-ing your fel-low men.
To Him who hath made them per-fect— Glo - ri - ous King of Kings.
Hast noth-ing to love? O tell me, Love you not God the Lord?

Noth-ing to love! Then has - ten! Go to the field and wood,
He is the lov - ing Shep - herd; Wan-der-ing sheep are we—
While there's an earth be - neath you, While there's a God a - bove,

And see if there's nought to love there, Nothing that's pure and good.
The earth is our pleas-ant pas-ture, Heav-en the fold shall be.
O, nev - er pro - fane them, saying, Noth-ing there is to love.

Words and Melody by J. R.

Harmonized by G. J. W.

MODERATO.

1 Thank-ful for the morn-ing light, Shin-ing o - ver earth and sea;
2. Thank-ful for the pow'r to hear, Thankful for the pow'r to speak;
3. Thanks I give for strength and health, Making all my puls-es leap;
4. Great-est boon is heart of love; May at length this heart be mine.

Thank-ful for the gift of sight, O Fa-ther, Lord, to Thee. To
Lord, to Thee I bend my ear, Thy ho - ly face I seek. To
Great-er boon than boundless wealth, Is wak-ing out of sleep. Con-
Lord, Thou sendest from a - bove Thy love and truth di - vine. And

Thee, with all the heart I pray, Now at the dawn-ing of the day.
Thee my ear-liest tho'ts are giv'n; Like in-cense, may they rise to heav'n,
tent, and glad for each new day, O, Fa-ther, Lord, to Thee I pray.
they shall purge the will ing soul Of earth-ly ills and make it whole.

I know Thou hast me in Thy care, And Thou wilt hear my pray'r.
And from thee thence a bless-ing bear, In an-swer to my pray'r.
I pray to heav'n, for Thou art there; And Thou art ev - 'ry-where.
For Thou didst come those ills to bear, And canst not spurn my pray'r.

Suffer Little Children.

Words and Melody by J. R.

Arranged by G. F. R.

ALLEGRETTO

1. "Let lit-tle chil-dren come to me," So says our bless ed Lord; And
2. "Let lit-tle chil-dren come to me," It is my Sav-ior's call; He
3. "Let lit-tle chil dren come to me," O, Fa-ther, Lord, I come; Thro'

I, a lit-tle child, must be O-be-dient to His word; On
spake it not to two or three, But to the chil-dren all; And
life and death I'll go with Thee, Thine arms shall be my home: I

Sab-bath days Must sing His praise, And bow be-fore Him, for He says,
so, when they His law o-bey, It is as if they heard Him say,
can-not fear When Thou art near; And Thy sweet words I seem to hear,

"Let lit-tle chil-dren come to me, Let lit-tle chil-dren come."
"Let lit-tle chil-dren come to me, Let lit-tle chil-dren come."
"Let lit-tle chil-dren come to me, Let lit-tle chil dren come."

Raindrops.

Words by J. R.

Music by G. F. R.

ALLEGRETTO

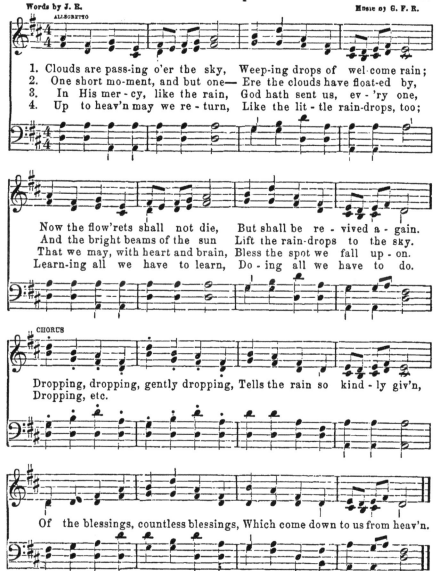

1. Clouds are pass-ing o'er the sky, Weep-ing drops of wel-come rain;
2. One short mo-ment, and but one— Ere the clouds have float-ed by,
3. In His mer - cy, like the rain, God hath sent us, ev - 'ry one,
4. Up to heav'n may we re - turn, Like the lit - tle rain-drops, too;

Now the flow'rets shall not die, But shall be re - vived a - gain.
And the bright beams of the sun Lift the rain-drops to the sky.
That we may, with heart and brain, Bless the spot we fall up - on.
Learn-ing all we have to learn, Do - ing all we have to do.

CHORUS

Dropping, dropping, gently dropping, Tells the rain so kind - ly giv'n,
Dropping, etc.

Of the blessings, countless blessings, Which come down to us from heav'n.

Festival Hymn.

O. F R.

1. Thou who in Thy church of old Sol - emn fes - ti - vals didst place,
2. Is - rael in the Promised Land Bless'd her God that brought her there.
3. Is - rael bless'd the God that sent Sinai's laws of strength and might,
4. Is - rael year-ly brought to mind Mem-ory of her wander-ings drear;
5. At thy fes - ti - vals, O. Lord, Thou didst bless the wait-ing hosts,

Smile on us thy lat - er fold; Come our fes - ti - val to grace!
Praise we now the lov - ing Hand That hath made our own so fair.
Thanks we bring that Thou hast lent For our guide, the gospel's light.
Year - ly still our spir - its find No con - tin-uing cit - y here.
Grant us now some quickening word, As of old at Pen - te - cost.

CHORUS

Come, O come to our hearts, Be - lov - ed Lord and King, In -

spire the prai - ses that we give, Ac - cept the thanks we bring.

Hark, the Skies.

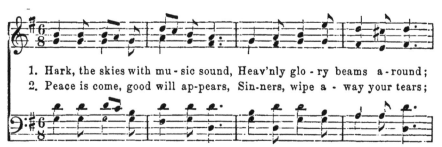

1. Hark, the skies with mu - sic sound, Heav'nly glo - ry beams a - round;
2. Peace is come, good will ap-pears, Sin-ners, wipe a - way your tears;

3 Shepherds, tending flocks by night, Heard the song and saw the light;
4. Mor-tals, hail the glo-rious King! Rich - est in-cense cheer-ful bring,
5. Glo - ry, praise, and bless-ing be, Lord, our Sav-ior un - to Thee;

Christ is born! the an - gels sing, Glo - ry to the new-born King.
Christ for you in flesh to - day, Humbly in the man-ger lay.

Took their reeds, and soft - est strains Ech-o'd thro' the hap - py plains.
Praise and love Im - man - uel's name, And His boundless grace proclaim.
Thee let heav'n and earth a - dore, God o'er all for - ev - er - more.

(59)

The Child and the Shepherd.

Composed for the "Welcome."

Words and Music by F. S.

NOT TOO FAST.

1. *Child.* O tell me, gen - tle shep - herd, gen - tle shep - herd, gen - tle
2. *Shepherd.* O lis - ten, hap - py chil - dren, hap - py chil - dren, hap - py
3. *Child.* O tell me, gen - tle shep - herd, gen - tle shep - herd, gen - tle
4. *Shepherd.* I will tell you, Chris - tian chil - dren, Chris - tian chil - dren, Chris - tian
5. *All.* Let us keep, then, hap - py Christ - mas, hap - py Christ - mas, hap - py

shep - herd, O tell me what the an - gel sang, In the
chil - dren, While I tell you what the an - gel sang, In the
shep - herd, What the great bright host of an - gels sang, All out
chil - dren, What the great bright host of an - gels sang, All out
Christ - mas, Chil - dren, shep - herds, men and an - gels, The blest

ear - ly Christ - mas morn. *Chorus.* O tell me what the
ear - ly Christ - mas morn. " Fear ye not, I bring good
in the fields so still. " What the great bright host of
in the fields so still. " "Glo - ry in the high - est,
song re - peat - ing still. " "Glo - ry in the high - est,

i Pedal

SLOW

an - gel sang, In the ear - ly Christ - mas morn.
ti - dings, For to - day the LORD is born!"
an - gels sang, All out in the fields so still.
glo - ry! Peace on earth, to men good will!"
glo - ry! Peace on earth, to men good will!"

1. Good Christian men, re-joice!   With heart, and soul, and voice;
2. Good Christian men, re-joice!   With heart, and soul, and voice;
3. Good Christian men, re-joice!   With heart, and soul, and voice;

Give ye heed to what we say; News! News! Christ, the Lord, is born to-day;
Now ye hear of endless bliss: Joy! Joy! Christ, the Lord, was born for this!
Now ye need not fear the grave: Peace! Peace! Christ, the Lord, was born to save!

Na-tions all be-fore Him bow, And He is in the man-ger now.
He hath oped the heav'nly door, And man is bless-ed ev-er-more.
Calls you one, and calls you all, To gain his ev-er-last-ing hall:

Christ is born to-day!   Christ is born to-day!
Christ was born for this!   Christ was born for this!
Christ was born to save!   Christ was born to save!

Carol, Brothers, Carol.

Melody and words by W. A. Muhlenberg, D. D.

Car - ol, brothers, car - ol,   Car - ol joy - ful - ly;

mf

Car - ol the good ti - dings,   Car - ol mer - ri - ly.

Car - ol, broth - ers, car - ol, Christ - mas day a - gain.

DUET. Andante. Note—The succeeding verses begin here.

1. Car - ol, but with glad - ness, Not in songs of earth;
2. At the mer - ry ta - ble, Think of those who've none,

On the Sav - ior's birth - day Hal - low'd be our mirth;
The or - phan and the wid - ow, Hun - gry and a - lone.

While a thous-and blessings   Fill our hearts with glee,
Boun - ti - ful your off'rings   To the al - tar bring;

D. C. CHORUS.

Christ-mas day we'll keep The   Feast of Char - i - ty.
Let the poor and need - y   Christ-mas car - ols sing.

3. List'ning angel music,
     Discord sure must cease;
   Who dare hate his brother
     On this day of peace?
   While the heav'ns are telling
     To mankind good will,
   Only love and kindness
     Every bosom fill.

4. Let our hearts, responding
     To the angel band,
   Wish this morning's sunshine
     Bright in every land.
   Word, and deed, and prayer
     Speed the grateful sound,
   Telling "Merry Christmas"
     All the world around.

The Christmas Tree.

Words by Rev. Dr. OGILBY.   By permission of Dr. H. S. CUTLER.

SOLO VOICE.

1. Our Christ-mas Tree is deck'd once more, In joy we meet a - round;
2. Our Christ-mas Tree is fresh and green, While skies are cold and drear;
3. Our Christ-mas Tree is shin - ing bright, While ev'n-ing shades sur-round;
4. Kind friends! whose hands have deck'd this tree, Our grateful thanks receive;

It tells of bright-er things in store; Let songs of praise re - sound.
Its har-vest store of fruit is seen, When win-ter blights the year.
Thus God doth give his chil-dren light, When dark-ness falls a - round.
Yet, Lord! for Christ-mas joys, to thee Our high-est praise we give.

CHORUS.

The Christ-mas Tree is an ev-er-green, It blooms when frost and

snow are seen; The Christ-mas tree is for-ev-er bright, It

shines with ev-er-last-ing light.

The Children's Hosanna.

Words by Rev. Dr. Ogilby.
By permission of Dr. H. S. Cutler.

SOLO VOICE.

1. Ho - san - na to King Da - vid's Son, De-
2. Ho - san - na to the new - born child, Of
3. Ho - san - na to th' in - carn - ate Word, In
4. With shep-herds on Ju - de - a's plains, With
5. Let ev - 'ry na - tion, ev - 'ry voice, In

scend - ed from the heav'n-ly throne; In Christ-mas songs we
vir - gin moth - er, meek and mild! In man - ger cra - dle
Beth-le'm born! the might - y God! Our hearts and tongues with
an - gels in their no - bler strains; Let our ho - san - nas
mer - ry Christ-mas songs re - joice; Both old and young with

hail his birth, Who brought sal - va - tion to the earth.
see Him laid, By whom the earth and heav'ns were made.
joy should raise Their glad ho - san - nas to his praise.
joy - ful rise To join the an - thems in the skies.
glad - ness sing, That Christ is born to be our King.

Morn of Joy.

Composed for the "Welcome."

Words and Music by F. S.

LIVELY AND JOYFUL

1. Morn of joy and morn of praise! Bright-est day of
2. Morn of glad - ness, morn of light! Fear and gloom are
3. O, what bright-ness from the Lord, Shines with - in His
4. Thith - er, too, O may we rise, When this earth - ly

all the days, For the Lord is ris - en, is
put to flight, For the Lord is ris - en, is
bless - ed Word, For the Lord is ris - en, is
bod - y dies,— Where our Lord is ris - en, is

ris - - en! Lo! they come at break of day,
ris - - en! Now no more the grave we fear,
ris - - en! Telling us of the world of light,
ris - - en! Strive we, then, in each new day,

AD LIB

Find the great stone roll'd a - way; Hark! and hear the
For we know "He is not here;" But the an - gel
Where there is no death nor night— Where, on Eas - ter
All that s wrong to put a - way; So shall we re-

an - gel say, The Lord, the Lord is ris - en, is
speaks good cheer, The Lord, the Lord is ris - en, is
morn - ing bright, The Lord, the Lord is ris - en, is
joic - ing say, The Lord, the Lord is ris - en, is

FULL CHORUS.

ris - - en. Al - le - - lu - ia! Al - le -
ris - - en. Al - le - - lu - ia! etc.
ris - - en. Al - le - - lu - ia! etc.
ris - - en. Al - le - - lu - ia! etc.

Pedal.

lu - ia! Al - le - lu - ia! Al - le - lu - ia!

Jesus is Risen.

From the "Service and Tune Book," by Hollister.

By permission of Mason Brothers, N. Y.

1. Je - sus is ris - en! Death is no more!
2. Break forth in sing - ing, O world new - born!
3. Chant Him, ye laughing flow'rs, Fresh from the sod;
4. Come where the Lord hath lain, Past is the gloom;

Lo! the white - rob - ed ones Sit by the door.
Chant the great Eas - ter - tide, Christ's ho - ly morn.
Chant Him, wild leap - ing streams, Prais - ing your God!
See the full eye of day Smile through the tomb.

mp

Dawn, gold - en morn - ing! Scat - ter the night!
Chant Him, young sun - beams, Danc - ing in mirth!
Break from *thy* win - ter, Sad heart, and sing!
Hark! an - gel voic - es Fall from the skies:

Haste, ye dis - ci - ples glad, First with the light;
Chant, all ye winds of God, Cours- ing the earth!
Bud with thy blossoms fair; Christ is thy spring.
Je - sus is ris - en! Glad heart, a - rise!

Dawn, gold - en morn - ing, Scat - ter the night!
Chant Him, young sun - beams, Danc - ing in mirth!
Break from *thy* win - ter, Sad heart, and sing!
Hark! an - gel voic - es Fall from the skies:

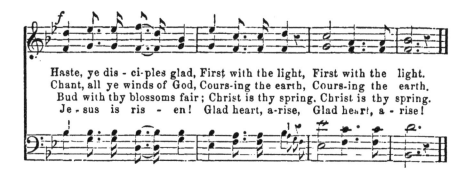

Haste, ye dis - ci - ples glad, First with the light, First with the light.
Chant, all ye winds of God, Cours-ing the earth, Cours-ing the earth.
Bud with thy blossoms fair; Christ is thy spring. Christ is thy spring.
Je - sus is ris - en! Glad heart, a-rise, Glad heart, a - rise!

PART V.

CHANTS, RESPONSES, ETC.

O, Sing unto the Lord.

B. R. H.

4. For the Lord is great, and greatly to be praised; he is to be feared a- | bove all | gods: } Praise ye the Lord.
5. For all the gods of the nations are idols; but the | Lord made the | heavens. } Praise ye the Lord.
6. Honor and majesty are before him; strength and beauty are | in his | sanctuary: } Praise ye the Lord in his holy temple.
7. Give unto the Lord, O ye kindreds of the people, give unto the Lord | glory and | strength: } Praise ye the Lord.
8. Give unto the Lord the glory due unto his name; bring an offering, and come in- | to his | courts: } Praise ye the Lord.
9. O, worship the Lord in the beauty of holiness; fear before him | all the | earth: } Praise ye the Lord in his holy temple.
10. Let the heavens rejoice, and let the] earth be | glad: Praise ye the Lord
11. Let the sea roar, and the | fullness there- | of: Praise ye the Lord.
12. Let the field be joyful, and all that | is there- | in: Praise ye the Lord in his holy temple
13. Then shall all the trees of the wood rejoice be- | fore the | Lord; } Praise ye the Lord.
14. For he cometh, for he cometh to | judge the | earth; Praise ye the Lord.
15. He shall judge the world with righteousness, and the | people with his | truth; (74) } Praise ye the Lord in his holy temple

[The teacher chants the verse; the children join in the response—"For his mercy," etc.]

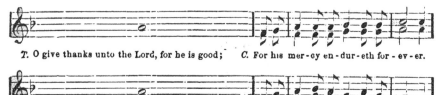

T. O give thanks unto the Lord, for he is good;   *C.* For his mer-cy en-dur-eth for-ev-er.

T.	O give thanks unto the God of gods;	C.	For his mercy, etc.
T.	O give thanks unto the Lord of lords;	C.	For his mercy, etc.
T.	To him who alone doeth great wonders;	C.	For his mercy, etc.
T.	To him that by wisdom made the heavens;	C.	For his mercy, etc.
T.	To him that stretched out the earth above the waters;	C.	For his mercy, etc.
T.	Who remembered us in our low estate;	C.	For his mercy, etc.
T.	And hath redeemed us from our enemies;	C.	For his mercy, etc.
T.	Who giveth food to all flesh;	C.	For his mercy, etc.
T.	O give thanks unto the God of Heaven;	C.	For his mercy, etc.

The Lord is Gracious.

1. The Lord is gracious and | full of com- | passion; ‖ slow to | anger and | of great | mercy.
2. The Lord is ; good to | all; ‖ and his mercies are | o-ver ; all his | works.
3. All thy works shall | praise thee, O ; Lord; ‖ and thy | saints shall | bless — ; thee.
4. They shall speak of the glory | of thy (kingdom; ‖ and | talk — ; of thy | power.
5. To make known to the sons of men his | mighty ; acts; ‖ and the glorious | majes-ty | of his | kingdom.
6. Thy kingdom is an ever- | last-ing | kingdom; ‖ and thy dominion endureth through- | out all | gen-er- | ations.

Holy, holy, holy.

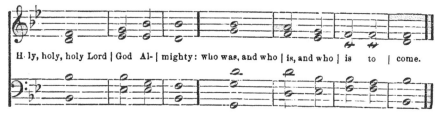

Ho-ly, holy, holy Lord | God Al- | mighty: who was, and who | is, and who | is   to | come.

Alleluia!—Psalm 113.

Al - le - lu - ia, Al - le - lu - ia, Al - le - lu - ia!

Teacher.   Children.

1.   O ye children   of the   Lord: Al - le - lu - ia!
       Praise the name   of the   Lord: Al - le - lu - ia!

2. *T.* Blessed be the name | of the | Lord: *C.* Alleluia!
     T. From this time forth and for- | ev-er- | more: *C.* Alleluia!
3. *T.* From the rising of the sun unto the going down | of the | same:
                                              C. Alleluia!

     T. The Lord's name is | to be | praised: *C.* Alleluia!
4. *T.* The Lord is high a- | bove all | nations: *C.* Alleluia!
     T. And his glory a- | bove the | heavens: *C.* Alleluia!
               Alleluia!   Alleluia!   Alleluia!

[The three closing Alleluias are to be sung like those at the beginning.]

Alleluia!—Psalm 148.

Al - le - lu - ia, Al - le - lu - ia, Al - le - lu - ia!

The small notes are for the Organist.

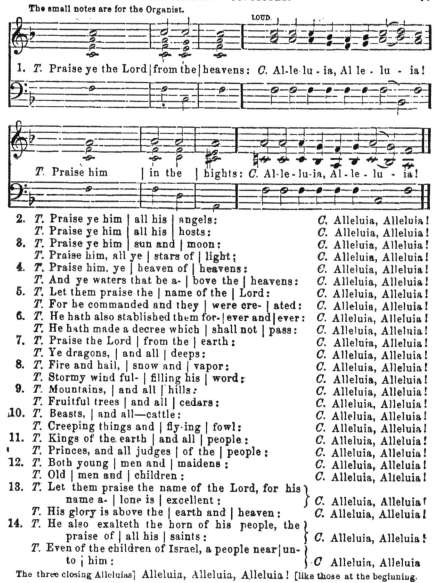

1. *T.* Praise ye the Lord | from the | heavens: *C.* Al-le-lu-ia, Al le - lu - ia!

T. Praise him | in the | hights: *C.* Al-le-lu-ia, Al-le-lu - ia!

2. *T.* Praise ye him | all his | angels:	*C.* Alleluia, Alleluia!
T. Praise ye him | all his | hosts:	*C.* Alleluia, Alleluia!
8. *T.* Praise ye him | sun and | moon:	*C.* Alleluia, Alleluia!
T. Praise him, all ye | stars of | light;	*C.* Alleluia, Alleluia!
4. *T.* Praise him. ye | heaven of | heavens:	*C.* Alleluia, Alleluia!
T. And ye waters that be a- | bove the | heavens:	*C.* Alleluia, Alleluia!
5. *T.* Let them praise the | name of the | Lord:	*C.* Alleluia, Alleluia!
T. For he commanded and they | were cre- | ated:	*C.* Alleluia, Alleluia!
6. *T.* He hath also stablished them for- | ever and | ever:	*C.* Alleluia, Alleluia!
T. He hath made a decree which | shall not | pass:	*C.* Alleluia, Alleluia!
7. *T.* Praise the Lord | from the | earth:	*C.* Alleluia, Alleluia!
T. Ye dragons, | and all | deeps:	*C.* Alleluia, Alleluia!
8. *T.* Fire and hail, | snow and | vapor:	*C.* Alleluia, Alleluia!
T. Stormy wind ful- | filling his | word:	*C.* Alleluia, Alleluia!
9. *T.* Mountains, | and all | hills:	*C.* Alleluia, Alleluia!
T. Fruitful trees | and all | cedars:	*C.* Alleluia, Alleluia!
10. *T.* Beasts, | and all—cattle:	*C.* Alleluia, Alleluia!
T. Creeping things and | fly-ing | fowl:	*C.* Alleluia, Alleluia!
11. *T.* Kings of the. earth | and all | people:	*C.* Alleluia, Alleluia!
T. Princes, and all judges | of the | people:	*C.* Alleluia, Alleluia!
12. *T.* Both young | men and | maidens:	*C.* Alleluia, Alleluia!
T. Old | men and | children:	*C.* Alleluia, Alleluia!
13. *T.* Let them praise the name of the Lord, for his name a- | lone is | excellent:	*C.* Alleluia, Alleluia!
T. His glory is above the | earth and | heaven:	*C.* Alleluia, Alleluia!
14. *T.* He also exalteth the horn of his people, the praise of | all his | saints:	*C.* Alleluia, Alleluia!
T. Even of the children of Israel, a people near | un-to | him:	*C.* Alleluia, Alleluia

The three closing Alleluias] Alleluia, Alleluia, Alleluia! [like those at the beginning.

First class of voices begin ; second class join in on upper notes; the others take the highest.

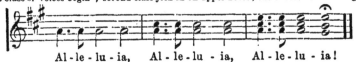

Al - le - lu - ia, Al - le - lu - ia, Al - le - lu - ia!

Small notes for the Organ.

1. Praise God in his sanc-tu - ary: Al - - le - lu - ia!

T. Praise him in the firmament of his power: *C.* Al - - le - lu - ia!

2. *T.* Praise him for his | might-y | acts;   *C.* Alleluia!
   T. Praise him according to his | excel-lent | greatness;   *C.* Alleluia!
3. *T.* Praise him with the | sound of the | trumpet;   *C.* Alleluia!
   T. Praise him with the | psaltery and | harp;   *C.* Alleluia!
4. *T.* Praise him with the | timbrel and | dance;   *C.* Alleluia!
   T. Praise him with stringed instru- | ments and | organs   *C.* Alleluia!
5. *T.* Praise him up- | on the loud | cymbals;   *C.* Alleluia!
   T. Praise him upon the high | sound-ing | cymbals;   *C.* Alleluia!
6. *T.* Let | ev-e-ry- | thing;   *C.* Alleluia!
   T. That hath breath | praise the | Lord;   *C.* Alleluia!

Alleluia, Alleluia, Alleluia!
[The three closing Alleluias like those at the beginning.]

My Soul doth Magnify.—LUKE 1 : 46.

GREGORIAN.

1. My soul doth magni- | fy the | Lord,
    And my spirit bath rejoiced in | God my | Sav- | ior:
2. For he hath regarded the low estate of | his hand- | maiden;
    For, behold, from henceforth, all generations shall | call me | bless- | ed
3. For he that is mighty hath done to | me great | things,
    And | ho-ly | is his | name.
4. And his mercy is on | them that | fear him,
    From generation to | gener- | a- | tions.
5. He hath showed | strength with his | arm;
    He hath scattered the proud in the imagin- | a-tion | of their | heart.
6. He hath put down the mighty | from their | seats,
    And exalted | them of | low de- | gree.
7. He hath filled the hungry | with good | things,
    And the rich he hath | sent | emp-ty a- | way.
8. He hath holpen his servant | Is-ra- | el,
    In re- | mem-brance | of his | mercy:
9. As he spake | to our | fathers,
    To Abraham, and to his | seed for- | ev- | er.

The Angels' Alleluia!—Rev. 19:6.

1. Alle | lu- | ia:
    For the Lord | God om- | nipo-tent | reigneth.
2. Let us be | glad and re- | joice,
    And give the | glo-ry | un-to | him:
3. For the marriage of the | Lamb is | come;
    And his | wife hath | made herself | ready.
4. And to her was granted that she should | be ar- | rayed
    In fine | lin-en, | bright and | clean:
5. For the | fine - | linen
    Is the | right-eous- | ness of | saints.
6. Blessed are | they that are | called
    Unto the marriage | sup-per | of the | Lamb.

Dox. Amen: Blessing, and | glo-ry, and | wisdom,
    And thanksgiving, and | hon-or, and | power, and | might,
    Be | unto our | God,
    For | ev-er and | ever: A- | men.   Rev. vii: 12.

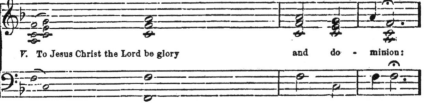

V. To Jesus Christ the Lord be glory   and   do -   minion:

For   ever and   ever: A -   men.

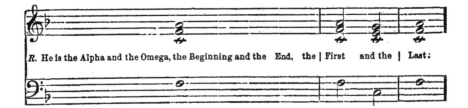

R. He is the Alpha and the Omega, the Beginning and the   End,   the | First   and the | Last;

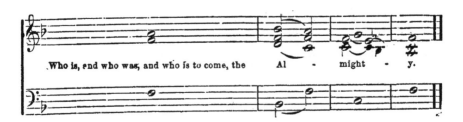

Who is, and who was, and who is to come, the   Al -   might -   y.

END OF THE MUSICAL PART.

SUGGESTIONS

REGARDING THE MANNER OF CONDUCTING THE SUNDAY-SCHOOL.

Behavior.—Every thing in the Sunday-school, whether in the order of exercises, or in the teacher's influence and example, or in the rules of conduct, should tend to the cultivation of reverence and obedience in the child. No loud talking or bois-terous behavior should ever be permitted in the Sunday-school room. If a child comes late, he should know that his tardy entrance disturbs all the others. No introductory exercises should be made use of as *mere pastimes* in the school to ac-commodate late-comers. Such a practice only cultivates in the children a careless disregard of rules and regulations, and destroys the solemn, religious impressions of the opening worship.

The Assembling.—It is desirable that on first assembling the whole school should, as far as practicable, be seated in one body, and not in separate classes, the opening exercises being those not of instruction but of united worship. Let the smaller children occupy the front seats, the larger ones being ranged in the seats behind, according to their sizes. The assistant teachers should have their regular seats among the children, and should see to the children's being properly seated, to finding their places in the Book, and otherwise keeping them in order and in readiness for the opening of the school by the superintendent or leader.

The Opening.—The duty and habit of looking to the Lord and asking his bless-ing at the beginning of whatever we undertake will be inculcated in the minds of the children by our beginning the school at once—or after an opening hymn—and the uttering of the Invitation, " Oh, come, let us worship," etc., by all kneeling down and uniting, with one voice, in the *Lord's Prayer;* after which may follow the responsive reading or singing of the Word; then a Hymn of Praise; and then some brief instruction addressed to the *whole school,* or some *common exercise* in the catechism or questions in some passage of the Word. The worship and *common lesson* being thus concluded, the children now separate into their proper classes under their respective teachers.

The Classes.—The classes are graded according to the age and capacity of the children. As many as ten or twelve children may be in one class. When there are too few in a class, the interest flags and the lesson becomes wearisome. About half an hour may be used in the class instruction. A part of this time should be used in training the class to *recite in concert* the answers in the catechism, or, when this is well learned, in repeating a psalm, or some other verses from the Word. The teacher should question the children familiarly about the *meaning* of every thing they recite. In infant classes a part of the time may be used in reading or telling a *carefully selected* story which shall convey a good and wholesome lesson; also in showing pictures illustrating the Bible, and asking questions about them. A series of text-books should be used in regular progression by the successive classes, and the children be thus enabled to constantly go forward from one grade of lessons to a higher.

The Catechism.—The catechism should be learned by all alike, old and young, being the first thing taught to every new-comer. The little children should learn it, by rote, one question at a time. The whole school should recite the catechism in concert as often as once a month. It would be well to make it the regular opening lesson for the whole school the first Sunday of every month. Great pains should be taken by the teachers in training the school to repeat the words distinctly, slowly, and loud enough to be heard by all, and in a rythmical and pleasing manner. The children should be taught to revere the Word and its truths, by uttering carefully and reverently their recitations.

Other Class-Lessons.—Besides the common training in the catechism, which older classes will soon have completed, the instruction of the separate classes may include the study of Bible-lessons, with the aid of maps and other illustrations; questions and answers on doctrinal subjects; the "Larger Catechism with Scripture Proofs;" the "Familiar Lessons for Sunday-Schools;" the "Doctrinal Class-Book;" "Illustrations of Scripture;" and the reading of some of the Writings of the Church, in course, from Sunday to Sunday, especially the "Four Leading Doctrines," the "True Christian Religion," and "Heaven and Hell."

The Closing.—The class-lessons being ended, the school comes together again in one body and all unite in singing such chants, hymns, or sacred songs as the time permits, concluding with the Dismissal Hymn, beginning "O most Merciful," page 25. Then let the children retire in an orderly procession, the little ones going before, led by their teachers, the older ones following in order. One child in each class or row of seats is appointed to see that the books are all neatly put away, the chairs, etc., arranged, so that the school-room, when left, is in perfect order and ready for the next time, or for any other service that may be held there. Work of this kind in the Sunday-school is to be regarded as a privilege, and will be cheerfully done by the children, who will at the same time learn habits of order, and feel the more interested in their school.

CHILDREN'S WORSHIP.

¶ *The children being all seated in one body, an opening hymn [page 10 to 19] may be sung. The Leader then says, the whole school rising promptly:*

O come let us worship and bow down:

Children. Let us kneel before the Lord our Maker.

Leader. For he is our God:

Children. And we are the people of his pasture, and the sheep of his hand.

¶ *All kneel down and say together aloud.*

Our Father who art in the heavens, hallowed be thy Name. Thy kingdom come. Thy will be done, as in heaven so also upon the earth. Give us this day our daily bread. And forgive us our debts, as we also forgive our debtors. And lead us not into temptation, but deliver us from evil. For thine is the kingdom, and the power, and the glory, forever. Amen.

The Leader. O Lord, open thou our lips:

Children. And our mouths shall show forth thy praise.

Here all stand up.

The Leader. Praise ye the Lord.

Children. The Lord's Name be praised.

All chant together the following Doxology: [Music on page 80.]

To JESUS CHRIST the LORD be glory | and do- | minion:

For- | ever and | ever. A- | men.

He is the Alpha and the Omega, the Beginning and the End, the | First and the | Last:

Who is, and who was, and who is to come, the | Al- | might- | y

(3)

¶ *Then the School repeats or chants with the Leader, or else by Divisions, in alter-*
nate verses, one of the following or other Psalms. Those too young to read
may learn the Psalm by rote and repeat it with the others.

Psalm 1.

1. Blessed is the man that walketh not in the counsel of the ungodly, nor standeth in the way of sinners, nor sitteth in the seat of
the scornful:

2. But his delight is in the law of the LORD; and in his law doth
he meditate day and night.

3. And he shall be like a tree planted by the rivers of water, that
bringeth forth his fruit in his season; his leaf also shall not wither;
and whatsoever he doeth shall prosper.

4. The ungodly are not so; but are like the chaff which the wind
driveth away.

5. Therefore the ungodly shall not stand in the judgment, nor
sinners in the congregation of the righteous.

6. For the LORD knoweth the way of the righteous; but the way
the ungodly shall perish.

Psalm 8.

1. O LORD our Lord, how excellent is thy name in all the earth!
who hast set thy glory above the heavens.

2. Out of the mouth of babes and sucklings hast thou ordained
strength because of thine enemies, that thou mightest still the enemy
and the avenger.

3. When I consider thy heavens, the work of thy fingers; the
moon and the stars, which thou hast ordained;

4. What is man, that thou art mindful of him? and the son of
man, that thou visitest him?

5. For thou hast made him a little lower than the angels, and hast
crowned him with glory and honor.

6. Thou madest him to have dominion over the works of thy hands; thou hast put all things under his feet.

7. All sheep and oxen, yea, and the beasts of the field;

8. The fowl of the air, and the fish of the sea, and whatsoever passeth through the paths of the seas.

9. O LORD our Lord, how excellent is thy name in all the earth!

PSALM 19.

1. The heavens declare the glory of God; and the firmament sheweth his handy work.

2. Day unto day uttereth speech, and night unto night sheweth knowledge.

3. There is no speech nor language, where their voice is not heard.

4. Their line is gone out through all the earth, and their words to the end of the world. In them hath he set a tabernacle for the sun,

5. Which is as a bridegroom coming out of his chamber, and rejoiceth as a strong man to run a race.

6. His going forth is from the end of the heaven, and his circuit unto the ends of it: and there is nothing hid from the heat thereof.

7. The law of the LORD is perfect, converting the soul: the testimony of the LORD is sure, making wise the simple.

8. The statutes of the LORD are right, rejoicing the heart; the commandment of the LORD is pure, enlightening the eyes.

9. The fear of the LORD is clean, enduring for ever: the judgments of the LORD are true and righteous altogether.

10. More to be desired are they than gold, yea, than much fine gold: sweeter also than honey and the honeycomb.

11. Moreover, by them is thy servant warned: and in keeping of them there is great reward.

12. Who can understand his errors? cleanse thou me from secret faults.

13. Keep back thy servant also from presumptuous sins; let them not have dominion over me: then shall I be upright, and I shall be innocent from the great transgression.

14. Let the words of my mouth, and the meditation of my heart, be acceptable in thy sight, O LORD, my strength, and my redeemer.

PSALM 23.

1. The LORD is my shepherd; I shall not want.

2. He maketh me to lie down in green pastures: he leadeth me beside the still waters.

3. He restoreth my soul: he leadeth me in the paths of righteousness for his name's sake.

4. Yea, though I walk through the valley of the shadow of death, I will fear no evil: for thou art with me; thy rod and thy staff they comfort me.

5. Thou preparest a table before me in the presence of mine enemies: thou anointest my head with oil; my cup runneth over.

6. Surely goodness and mercy shall follow me all the days of my life: and I will dwell in the house of the LORD forever.

PSALM 67.

1. God be merciful unto us, and bless us; and cause his face to shine upon us.

2. That thy way may be known upon earth, thy saving health among all nations.

3. Let the people praise thee, O God; let all the people praise thee.

4. O let the nations be glad and sing for joy; for thou shalt judge the people righteously, and govern the nations upon earth.

5. Let the people praise thee, O God; let all the people praise thee.

6. Then shall the earth yield her increase; and God, even our own God, shall bless us.

7. God shall bless us, and all the ends of the earth shall fear him.

PSALM 91.

1. He that dwelleth in the secret place of the Most High shall abide under the shadow of the Almighty.

2. I will say of the LORD, He is my refuge and my fortress: my God; in him will I trust.

3. Surely he shall deliver thee from the snare of the fowler, and from the noisome pestilence.

4. He shall cover thee with his feathers, and under his wings shalt thou trust; his truth shall be thy shield and buckler.

5. Thou shalt not be afraid for the terror by night; nor for the arrow that flieth by day;

6. Nor for the pestilence that walketh in darkness; nor for the destruction that wasteth at noonday.

7. A thousand shall fall at thy side, and ten thousand at thy right hand; but it shall not come nigh thee.

8. Only with thine eyes shalt thou behold and see the reward of the wicked.

9. Because thou hast made the LORD which is my refuge, even the Most High, thy habitation;

10. There shall no evil befall thee, neither shall any plague come nigh thy dwelling.

11. For he shall give his angels charge over thee, to keep thee in all thy ways.

12. They shall bear thee up in their hands, lest thou dash thy foot against a stone.

13. Thou shalt tread upon the lion and adder: the young lion and the dragon shalt thou trample under feet.

. 14. Because he hath set his love upon me, therefore will I deliver him: I will set him on high, because he hath known my name.

. 15. He shall call upon me, and I will answer him; I will be with him in trouble; I will deliver him and honor him,

16. With long life will I satisfy him, and shew him my salvation.

PSALM 103.

1. Bless the LORD, O my soul: and all that is within me, bless his holy name.

2. Bless the LORD, O my soul, and forget not all his benefits:

3. Who forgiveth all thine iniquities; who healeth all thy diseases;

4. Who redeemeth thy life from destruction; who crowneth thee with loving-kindness and tender mercies;

5. Who satisfieth thy mouth with good things; so that thy youth is renewed like the eagle's.

6. The LORD executeth righteousness and judgment for all that are oppressed.

7. The LORD hath prepared his throne in the heavens; and his kingdom ruleth all.

8. Bless the LORD, ye his angels, that excel in strength, that do his commandments, hearkening unto the voice of his word.

9. Bless ye the LORD, all ye his hosts; ye ministers of his, that do his pleasure.

10. Bless the LORD, all his works in all places of his dominion: bless the Lord, O my soul.

PSALM 119.

1. Wherewithal shall a young man cleanse his way? By taking heed thereto according to thy word.

2. With my whole heart have I sought thee: O let me not wander from thy commandments.

3. Thy word have I hid in my heart, that I might not sin against thee.

4. Blessed art thou, O LORD: teach me thy statutes.

5. With my lips have I declared all the judgments of thy mouth.

6. I have rejoiced in the way of thy testimonies, as much as in all riches.

7. I will meditate in thy precepts, and have respect unto thy ways.

8. I will delight myself in thy statutes: I will not forget thy word.

PSALM 119, v. 105.

1. Thy word is a lamp unto my feet, and a light unto my path.

2. I have sworn, and I will perform it, that I will keep thy righteous judgments.

3. I am afflicted very much: quicken me, O LORD, according unto thy word.

4. Accept, I beseech thee, the freewill-offerings of my mouth, O LORD, and teach me thy judgments.

5. My soul is continually in my hand: yet do I not forget thy law.

6. The wicked have laid a snare for me: yet I erred not from thy precepts.

7. Thy testimonies have I taken as a heritage for ever: for they are the rejoicing of my heart.

8. I have inclined my heart to perform thy statutes always, even unto the end.

PSALM 121.

1. I will lift up mine eyes unto the hills, from whence cometh my help.

2. My help cometh from the LORD, which made heaven and earth.

3. He will not suffer thy foot to be moved: he that keepeth thee will not slumber.

4. Behold, he that keepeth Israel shall neither slumber nor sleep

5. The LORD is thy keeper: the LORD is thy shade upon thy right hand.

6. The sun shall not smite thee by day, nor the moon by night.

7. The LORD shall preserve thee from all evil: he shall preserve thy soul.

8. The LORD shall preserve thy going out and thy coming in from this time forth, and even for evermore.

PSALM 122.

1. I was glad when they said unto me, Let us go into the house of the LORD.

2. Our feet shall stand within thy gates, O Jerusalem.

3. Jerusalem is builded as a city that is compact together:

4. Whither the tribes go up, the tribes of the LORD, unto the testimony of Israel, to give thanks unto the name of the LORD.

5. For there are set thrones of judgment, the thrones of the house of David.

6. Pray for the peace of Jerusalem: they shall prosper that love thee.

7. Peace be within thy walls, and prosperity within thy palaces.

8. For my brethren and companions' sakes, I will now say, Peace be within thee.

9. Because of the house of the LORD our God I will seek thy good.

¶ *The Psalm being ended, the whole school unite in singing, " To God the Father, Spirit, Son," on page* 20, *or else some other suitable Hymn of praise.*

The school being seated, the leader may read a passage from the Word presenting a single precept, parable, miracle, or other interesting narrative, and question the children on what has been read. Or he may give them some other short instruction addressed to the whole school alike. On the first Sunday of each month, let the whole school recite the catechism through in concert. The general instruction being ended, another hymn may be sung (if there be time), and then the children go to their respective classes for their class lessons. These being ended, the school assembles again in one body, and a number of chants, hymns, or sacred songs are sung according as the time permits, closing always with the dismissal hymn, "O most Merciful," etc., page 25.

THE FIRST QUESTIONS.

¶ IT will be well, especially in mission schools or where children attend whose parents are not of the Church, to impress upon their minds the grand distinctive doctrine of the New Church by asking the whole school, from time to time, the following or similar questions:

Teacher. What Sunday-school is this?

Children. The New Church Sunday-school.

T. What is the New Church called in the Bible?

C. The New Jerusalem.

T. What is the first thing the New Church Sunday-school teaches you?

C. That there is One God.

T. And who is He?

C. The LORD JESUS CHRIST.

T. And what is the second great truth the New Church teaches you?

C. That to be saved, we must keep the commandments.

T. And what, in brief, are the commandments?

C. We must love the LORD with our whole heart, and our neighbor as ourselves.

T. Can you do this?

C. With the LORD's help we can.

T. How do you ask the LORD to help you?

C. By praying to Him.

T. How do you pray to Him?

C. Our Father who art in the heavens, hallowed be thy Name. Thy kingdom come. Thy will be done, as in heaven so also upon the earth. Give us this day our daily bread. And forgive us our debts, as we also forgive our debtors. And lead us not into temptation; but deliver us from evil. For thine is the kingdom, and the power, and the glory forever. Amen.

THE CATECHISM,

Being the "Child's First Catechism" of the Conference of the New Church in England.

Question. Who made you and keeps you alive?

Answer. Our Father in heaven.

Q. What else has He made?

A. He has made the heavens and the earth, all people and all things.

Q. By what other names is our Father in heaven called?

A. He is called God, the Lord, Jehovah, the Lord Jesus Christ, and by many other names.

Q. Why did God make you?

A. That I might do good while I live in this world, and go to heaven when I die.

Q. Do all people go to heaven when they die?

A. Only those who are good.

Q. What is heaven?

A. Heaven is the world above, full of all beautiful things, where God dwells. It is the home of the angels, where they live in love, and are happy, near to their heavenly Father.

Q. If you are not good, what will become of you?

A. I shall become a wicked spirit when I die, and live in hell forever.

Q. What is hell?

A. Hell is the lower world, full of ugly and wretched things, where the wicked spirits live in hatred and misery, with their hearts turned away from their heavenly Father.

Q. If you wish to be good, what must you do?

A. I must pray to the Lord Jesus Christ to help me to be good and to grow better; I must always speak the truth, obey my parents, try to learn my duty, and be kind to every body.

Q. How are you to learn what is your duty?

A. I must read the Word of God, and do what it tells me, and try to be as useful as I can.

Q. What does the Word of God teach you?

A. Two things: my duty to God, and my duty to my neighbor.

Q. What is your duty to God?

A. God tells us in His Word, "Thou shalt love the Lord thy God with all thy heart, and with all thy soul, and with all thy mind."

Q. What must you do to show that you love God?

A. I must shun every thing that is wrong, because it is a sin against God; and I must do every thing that is right, because it is pleasing to Him.

Q. You said the Bible teaches you your duty to your neighbor; who is your neighbor?

A. Every one; but, most of all, those to whom I can be kind and useful.

Q. What is your duty to your neighbor?

A. The Lord teaches us in the Bible, "Thou shalt love thy neighbor as thyself."

Q. How can you show that you love your neighbor as yourself?

A. By doing what is right to him at all times.

Q. Where do you learn what is right?

A. In the Ten Commandments.

Q. Can you say them?

A. God spake all these words, saying:

I. I AM the LORD thy God who have brought thee forth out of the land of Egypt, out of the house of bondage. Thou shalt have no other gods before me. Thou shalt not make unto thee any graven image, or any likeness of any thing that is in heaven above, or that is in the earth beneath, or that is in the water under the earth: thou shalt not bow down thyself to them nor serve them: for I the LORD thy God am a jealous God, visiting the iniquity of the fathers upon the children unto the third and fourth generation of them that hate me; and showing mercy unto thousands of them that love me and keep my commandments.

II. Thou shalt not take the name of the LORD thy God in vain: for the LORD will not hold him guiltless that taketh His name in vain.

III. Remember the Sabbath day, to keep it holy. Six days shalt thou labor, and do all thy work: but the seventh day is the Sabbath of the LORD thy God: in it thou shalt not do any work, thou, nor thy son, nor thy daughter, thy man-servant, nor thy maid-servant, nor thy cattle, nor thy stranger that is within thy gates: for in six days the LORD made heaven and earth, the sea, and all that in them is, and rested the seventh day: wherefore the LORD blessed the Sabbath day, and hallowed it.

IV. Honor thy father and thy mother: that thy days may be long upon the land which the LORD thy God giveth thee.

V. Thou shalt not kill.

VI. Thou shalt not commit adultery.

VII. Thou shalt not steal.

VIII. Thou shalt not bear false witness against thy neighbor.

IX. Thou shalt not covet thy neighbor's house.

X. Thou shalt not covet thy neighbor's wife, nor his man-servant, nor his maid-servant, nor his ox, nor his ass, nor any thing that is thy neighbor's.

Q. Can you keep these commandments?

A. Not without the Lord's help; but He has promised to help me, if I ask Him.

Q. How should you ask Him to help you?

A. By praying to Him.

Q. When ought you to pray to the Lord?

A. Every morning and evening, and whenever else I need His help.

Q. What ought you to say when you pray?

A. The best prayer is the Lord's Prayer.

Q. Let me hear you say it.

OUR Father who art in the heavens, hallowed be thy Name. Thy kingdom come. Thy will be done, as in heaven, so also upon the earth. Give us this day our daily bread. And forgive us our debts, as we also forgive our debtors. And lead us not into temptation; but deliver us from evil. For thine is the kingdom, and the power, and the glory, forever. Amen.

OF THE LORD.

Q. What ought you to think about the Lord?

A. That He is the one only God, in whom is the Divine Trinity of Father, Son, and Holy Spirit.

Q. What else do you know about the Lord?

A. That He is all-loving, all-wise, and almighty.

Q. When we speak of God, of whom are we to think?

A. Of the Lord Jesus Christ, who is "the only wise God our Savior."

Q. Why is the Lord Jesus Christ called God?

A. Because he made all things, and keeps all things in being.

Q. Why is God also called our Savior?

A. Because God came down into this world to save men. He was born as a little child, and was named Jesus Christ; He suffered, was crucified, rose from the dead, and is "over all, God blessed for ever-more."

Q. Then to whom ought we to pray?

A. We ought always to pray to the Lord Jesus Christ, because He is the everlasting Father, "the First and the Last, the Almighty."

OF THE SACRED SCRIPTURE.

Q. What is that book called, which contains the words of the Lord?

A. The Word of God, The Sacred Scripture, and The Holy Bible.

Q. Why is it called Sacred and Holy?

A. Because God caused the writers to set down exactly what He told them, so that even the words are holy, because they came from God.

Q. Whom is the Bible intended to teach?

A. Men, women, and children on earth, and also the angels in heaven.

Q. For what purpose was it given?

A. To teach us what is the will of the Lord, what we ought to do, and how we ought to live, and to tell us about heaven.

Q. Is it not your duty, then, to read and understand it?

A. Yes; I ought to read some of it every day, and ask the Lord to help me to understand it, as well as to help me to do what it tells me.

Q. What are the chief truths of faith taught you in the Bible?

A. They are these:

1. That God is one, in whom is a Divine Trinity, and that He is the Lord God and Savior JESUS CHRIST.

2. That a saving faith is to believe on Him.

3. That evil actions ought not to be done, because they are of the devil, and from the devil.

4. That good actions ought to be done, because they are of God, and from God.

5. And that they should be done by man as of himself; nevertheless under this belief, that they are from the Lord, operating with him and by him.

THE END OF THE CATECHISM.

QUESTIONS IN BIBLE HISTORY AND GEOGRAPHY.

PART I. THE OLD TESTAMENT.

A map showing the "Lands of the Bible" is displayed before the school; or else the class is provided with convenient hand maps for their own use. Every one has a Bible, and when the teacher names the reference the class immediately turn to it and find the proper answer to the question. Or, the references may be studied at home, and the questions answered in the class from memory. The teacher should not confine his questions to those here given, but invent as many others as possible; particularly should he endeavor to draw out all the interesting and striking points of the passages referred to in the Word. An excellent and very useful book of maps, with tables of dates, names, weights and measures, etc., is the "Bible Atlas and Gazetteer," published by the American Tract Society.

Teacher. What is this a map of?

What sea is this? (*pointing to the Mediterranean.*)

What country is this, east of the Mediterranean?

What country lies south of it? (*pointing to Egypt.*)

What was the ancient name of Palestine? *Ans.* Canaan.

Who came to live there? *Ans.* Abraham.

Where did he come from? *Ans.* Ur of the Chaldees. Gen. xi, xii.

What direction was that from Canaan? *Ans.* East.

Where did Abraham live? *Ans.* Hebron. (*Point it out.*)

Who were Abraham's descendants? *Ans.* Isaac and Jacob.

What was Jacob's other name? Gen. xxxii.

Where did Jacob live? Gen. xxxv: 27.

How many children had Jacob or Israel?

Can you name them? Rev. vii: 4. Exodus i.

What can you tell me about Joseph? Gen. xxxvii.

Where did Joseph go to seek his brethren? Where did he find them?

Did Joseph's brethren and his father all come down to Egypt? Gen. xlii–xlvi.

Point out where Egypt is.

What did they do in Egypt? Gen. xlvii.

At length, when Pharaoh oppressed them, whom did the Lord send to deliver the Israelites? Exodus iii.

On what night did they go out of Egypt? Exodus xii.

What happened that night in the houses of the Egyptians? v. 29, 30.

How did the Israelites escape? v. 23.

What is this night of deliverance called? *Ans.* The Passover, v. 27

How was it to be commemorated? *Ans.* By the yearly feast of the Passover.

What do we read in the Commandments about this our deliverance from Egypt?

Did our Lord ever go down into Egypt? Matt. ii. Why? And what prophecy was thus fulfilled? *Ans.* "Out of Egypt have I called my son."

Did our Lord ever keep the Passover? Luke xxii.

With whom? Where?

Now tell me again what the Passover was to commemorate? *Ans.* That the Lord "has brought us up out of the land of Egypt, out of the house of bondage."

I.

When the children of Israel escaped from Egypt, what city did they go out from? Exodus xii: 37.

How did the Lord lead them?

What sea did they come to? Ex. xiv.

How did they cross it?

Did Pharaoh pursue them?

What became of him and his hosts?

Point out Rameses and the Red Sea.

After crossing the Red Sea where did they go? xv: 22–27.

What did they find at Marah?

What did they find at Elim?

How many wells? How many palm-trees?

Now can any one tell me,—

How many apostles did our Lord choose? Luke vi: 13.

How many other disciples did He send out to preach? Luke x: 1.

Are these numbers the same as those of the wells and palm-trees at Elim?

Point out, on the map, Elim and Marah.

Where did they come in the third month? Exodus xix.

What took place on Mount Sinai?

Where is Mount Sinai?

Can you trace the journeying of the Israelites in the wilderness? See Numbers xxxiii. [Map II in the "Bible Atlas and Gazetteer."]

How many years were they wandering in the wilderness? Deut. viii: 2.

How many days was our Lord tempted of the devil? Luke iv: 1, 2.

Did Moses go with the Israelites into Canaan? Deut. xxxi.

Who became their leader now?

Where did Moses die? Deut. xxxiv.

Point out Mount Nebo.

What river must they cross to come into Canaan?

How did they cross it? Joshua iii, iv.

What city did they now besiege? vi.

Point out Jericho.

How did they take it? Josh. vi.

At length, when the Israelites had driven out the Canaanites, did they inherit the whole land of Canaan?

What was their great capital city? *Ans.* Jerusalem.

What great king ruled here over all Israel? *Ans.* David.

What great sacred building was here? *Ans.* The Temple.

Who built the Temple? *Ans.* King Solomon.

Whose son was Solomon? *Ans.* David's.

Afterward was the kingdom divided? *Ans.* Yes, into the two king-doms of Judah and Israel.

Was Jerusalem at length destroyed and the Jews taken captive? *Ans.* Yes, by Nebuchadnezzar, King of Babylon.

And where were the Jews carried away captive? *Ans.* To Babylon.

Where is Babylon?

But did they ever return again and rebuild Jerusalem? *Ans.* Yes, in the reign of Cyrus, King of the Persians.

What nation afterward got possession of Palestine? *Ans.* The Romans.

To what empire did Judea belong at the time our Lord was born? *Ans.* The Roman Empire.

Who was then Emperor of Rome? *Ans.* Cæsar Augustus.

And who was King of Judea? *Ans.* Herod.

PART II. THE NEW TESTAMENT.

The class have before them a map of Palestine showing distinctly the River Jor-dan, the Dead Sea, the Sea of Galilee, and the boundary lines of Judea, Samaria, and Galilee. If the teacher can draw an outline map in the presence of the class, using a small map for a guide, and putting in the various localities in the order in which they are taken up in the questions, it will add much to the usefulness and pleasure of the exercise.

What country is this a map of?

By what other name do we call Palestine? *Ans.* The Holy Land.

Why do we call it so? *Ans.* Because our Lord lived there.

What sea is the Holy Land east of?

What river borders the Holy Land on the east?

What lake or sea does the Jordan flow from?

And into what?

Into what three countries was Palestine divided in the time of our Lord? *Ans.* Judea, Samaria, Galilee.

Which was the most northern?

What was this called?   *Ans.* Galilee of the Gentiles.

Which was the most southern division?

And what country lay between Galilee and Judea?

How is Judea bounded?

How is Samaria bounded?

How is Galilee bounded?

What great mountains are north of Galilee?   *Ans.* The mountains of Lebanon.

Where did the angel appear to Zacharias, the father of John the Baptist?   Luke i.

Where was the Temple?

On what mount in Jerusalem?   *Ans.* Mount Moriah.

Describe the different parts of the Temple.   (*Show a map of the Temple.*)

What was in the Holy of Holies?

What was in the Holy place?

What was outside of the Holy place?

Where was the angel standing when seen by Zacharias?   Luke i, 11.

Point out the altar of incense.

What was kept in the Ark of the Covenant?   Exodus xl.

What was the "Testimony?"   *Ans.* The Ten Commandments

What was over the ark?

What hung before it?

Where did Joseph and Mary live?   *Ans.* At Nazareth.

In what country is Nazareth?   Point it out.

Whither did Joseph and Mary go to be taxed?

Where was our Lord born?   Luke ii.

In what country is Bethlehem?   Point it out.

What direction from Jerusalem?   From Hebron?   About how far from these places?

Is Bethlehem in the "Hill country?"

What is that part of Judea called which is about the Dead Sea?
Ans. The wilderness of Judea.

Where did they bring the Lord after some days?   Luke ii.

Who saw Him there in the temple, and rejoiced and gave thanks?

Who was the Roman Emperor when the Lord was born?

Who was the King of Judea?   Matthew ii.

Where did the wise men come from?

Whom did they wish to find?

To what city did they come?

Then where did they go?

What did they present to the Lord?

Where did Joseph now go with the young child and His mother?

In what direction is Egypt?

And when they returned from Egypt where did they go to live?

Where, then, was Jesus' home, when a boy?

When Jesus was twelve years old where did he go with his parents?
Luke ii.

Point out the journey.

Tell what took place in Jerusalem.

Where did John the Baptist come preaching?   Luke iii.

Where did he baptize the people?   John i: 28.

Point out Bethabara.

Where was our Lord baptized?   Matt. iii.

By whom?

Where was our Lord tempted?   Matt. iv.

How many days?

How many years were the Israelites tempted in the wilderness?

Who came and ministered to the Lord after His temptation?

Where did our Lord now go to live?

What prophecy was fulfilled?

Where did he call His twelve apostles?

What was their occupation?

Point out the Sea of Galilee.

Where did our Lord now go about doing good?

And what people came to Him and followed Him?

II.

OUR LORD IN GALILEE.

Name some of the places in Galilee where our Lord went. *Ans.* Nazareth, Cana, Nain, Capernaum, Bethsaida, Magdala, the Sea of Galilee, the country of the Gadarenes, Cæsarea Philippi.

Point out these places.

What mountain is near to Nain?

What great mountain is near to Cæsarea Philippi?

What do we read in the Psalms about these mountains? Psalms lxxxix : 12.

Now find Cana, and tell me what took place there? John ii, iv: 46.

Find Capernaum. What took place there? Mark i : 21 ; ii: 1–14; iii. Matt. v, viii, ix: 27–34. John vi: 22. Matt. xvii: 24. Mark v: 22.

Did our Lord visit again the place where He had lived as a child? Matt. iv: 13. Mark vi: 1–6.

What place was it? How did the people receive Him there?

Point out Nain. What did our Lord here? Luke vii: 11.

What did our Lord at Bethsaida (Julias)? Mark viii: 22.

Where is Bethsaida (Julias)?

Where was our Lord going?

Point out Cæsarea Philippi.

What took place near Bethsaida? Luke ix: 10.

Did our Lord visit Tyre and Sidon? Mark vii: 24.

Point out these places.

Where did He then go? v. 31.

By what other name was the Sea of Galilee called? *Ans.* The Sea of Tiberias. John vi: 1.

What towns are on the shore of the Sea of Galilee?

What took place on the Sea of Galilee?   Matt. viii: 18; xiv: 22; xxviii: 16.

What took place on the shore of this lake?   Mark iv.

What took place on the other side of the lake?   Luke viii: 26.

III.

Our Lord in Samaria and beyond Jordan.

When our Lord went from Galilee up to Jerusalem what country must He pass through?

At what great festival did our Lord go up to Jerusalem?   *Ans.* At the "Feast of the Passover."

What took place once when He was returning from Jerusalem as He passed through Samaria?   John iv: 4.

At what place was the well where He stopped to rest?

Whose well was it?   Who was Jacob?

What was the old name of Sychar?   *Ans.* Schechem.

What other name has this place?   *Ans.* Neapolis.

Point it out.

What took place another time as He was passing through Samaria on His way to Jerusalem?   Luke ix: 51; xvii: 11.

Did our Lord ever visit the country on the other side of the Jordan?   Matt. xix: 1.

What was that country called?   *Ans.* Perea.

What did He do there?

IV.

Our Lord at and near Jerusalem.

Point out Jerusalem.   (*Show the class a map of Jerusalem and its surroundings.*)

On what two famous hills is the city built? *Ans.* On Mount Zion and Mount Moriah.

What was Mount Zion called? *Ans.* The City of David.

What great building was on Mount Moriah?

Name the places about Jerusalem, and point them out. The Brook Kidron; Valley of Jehosaphat; the Pool of Siloam; the Mount of Olives; Bethany and Bethphage; Emmaus; Jericho; the Jordan; the road to Bethany; the road to Emmaus; the Garden of Gethsemane; the supposed site of Calvary or place where our Lord was crucified and buried.

On what occasions did our Lord come up to Jerusalem? *Ans.* At the Feast of the Passover; also at the Feast of the Tabernacles (John vii), and at the Feast of the Dedication (John x).

In what month was the Passover? *Ans.* Abib.

This corresponds to what month in our calendar? *Ans.* April.

When was the Feast of Tabernacles? *Ans.* In October.

And when the Feast of the Dedication? *Ans.* On the 25th of December.

Point out Jericho; what took place here? Luke xix.

Point out the Pool of Siloam; what took place there? John ix.

Point out Bethany. What mountain is between Bethany and Jerusalem?

About how far is Bethany from Jerusalem?

Who lived in Bethany? John xi: 1.

Did our Lord often visit there?

Tell me of these visits, and what He did there. Luke x: 38. John xi, xii. Matt. xxvi.

Tell me what took place on the Mount of Olives. Matt. xxiv: 3.

What took place in the Temple in Jerusalem? Luke xxi: 1–14. Matt. xxi: 12.

What took place on the road from Bethany to Jerusalem? Matt. xxi.

Where did our Lord keep the Passover with His disciples? Matt. xxvi: 17.

By what other name was the Passover called? *Ans.* "The Feast of unleavened bread."

When was this Feast of the Passover instituted?

To commemorate what?

Was it in the evening that the Lord kept the Passover with the twelve?

After the Supper what did they? Matt. xxvi: 30.

Where did they go then?

Was it night?

What brook must they cross to go from Jerusalem to the Mount of Olives? John xviii: 1.

What garden did they enter?

Can you point out the Brook Kidron and the Garden of Gethsemane?

On the side of what mountain is this garden?

What did our Lord in the Garden of Gethsemane?

Who now came out from the city to take Him?

Who betrayed Him?

Where did they bring our Lord?

And from the high priest's palace they lead Him where? Matt. xxvii. John xviii: 28.

And where did they crucify Him? John xix: 17.

What is Golgotha also called? *Ans.* Calvary. Luke xxiii: 33.

And where did Joseph and Nicodemus bury the body of our Lord? John xix: 38.

And when our Lord was risen from the dead on the morning of the first day of the week, who saw Him first? John xx: 11.

Did our Lord appear, after His resurrection, to His disciples?

What took place on the road to Emmaus? Luke xxiv: 13.

Where did our Lord tell His disciples to go and meet Him, after His resurrection? Matt. xxviii: 9, 16.

Did our Lord appear to His disciples in Galilee as He had prom-ised? John xxi.

For how many days after His resurrection did our Lord show Him-self to His disciples here on earth? *Ans.* During forty days. Acts i.

And after that whither did our Lord go? *Ans.* He ascended up to heaven.

Where did His ascension take place? Luke xxiv: 50.

Where did our Lord instruct His disciples to remain? Luke xxiv: 49.

Until He should send them what?

Did they accordingly wait in Jerusalem as He had instructed them? v. 52.

How long did they remain there? *Ans.* Until the day of Pente-cost (Acts ii), when they were filled with the Holy Ghost, and began to preach the Gospel, and to baptize all nations into the name of the Lord Jesus: to whom be glory and dominion forever! Amen.

THE END.

THE SCRIPTURE ALPHABET.

Let the little children learn the following sentences, one at a time, in their alphabetical order, and then recite them, in their class, in turn.

ALL thy works shall praise thee, O Lord, and thy saints shall bless thee.

BLESSED is the man that feareth the Lord, that delighteth greatly in His commandments.

COME unto me, all ye that labor and are heavy laden, and I will give you rest.

DEPART from evil and do good: seek peace and pursue it.

ENTER into His gates with thanksgiving, and into His courts with praise.

FRET not thyself because of evil-doers; neither be thou envious against the workers of iniquity.

GIVE me understanding and I shall keep thy law: yea, I shall observe it with my whole heart.

HAVE mercy upon me, O God, according to thy loving-kindness.

IN thee, O Lord, do I put my trust; let me never be ashamed.

JUSTICE and judgment are the habitation of thy throne.

KEEP thy tongue from evil, and thy lips from speaking guile.

LIGHT is sown for the righteous, and gladness for the upright in heart.

MANY are the afflictions of the righteous, but the Lord delivereth him out of them all.

NOT unto us, O Lord, not unto us, but unto thy name give glory.

OPEN thou mine eyes, O Lord, that I may behold wondrous
things out of thy law.

PRAY for the peace of Jerusalem: they shall prosper that love
thee.

QUICKEN me after thy loving-kindness: so shall I keep the testimony of thy mouth.

REST in the Lord, and wait patiently for Him.

SIX days shalt thou labor and do all thy work: but the seventh
day is the Sabbath of the Lord thy God.

THY Word is a lamp unto my feet, and a light unto my path.

UNTO thee, O God, do we give thanks; for that thy name is near
thy wondrous works declare.

VERILY there is a reward for the righteous; verily He is a God
that judgeth in the earth.

WHEREWITHAL shall a young man cleanse his way? by taking heed thereto according to thy Word.

XCEPT the Lord keep the city: the watchman waketh but in
vain.

YE that fear the Lord trust in the Lord: He is their help and
their shield.

ZION heard and was glad; and the daughters of Judah rejoiced
because of thy judgments, O Lord.

THE CHAIN OF GOLDEN WORDS,

Or fifty-two precious sentences from the Holy Word, to be learned, one on each succeeding Sunday throughout the year, and to be recited entire at the year's end. An exercise for the younger classes.

NOTE.—The Chain is held together (in the memory) in this way: the first letter of the closing word of each sentence is the letter with which the following sentence begins. The "Chain" may be recited by the whole school, at the end of the year, each child reciting his sentence in its turn.

THE CHAIN.

1st *Sunday of the year.* The Lord is good to all.

2d   "   All thy works praise thee.

3d   "   Thy Word is true from the beginning.

4th   "   Blessed are they that hear the Word of God and do it.

5th   "   In thee, O Lord, do I put my trust.

6th   "   Trust in the Lord, and do good.

7th   "   God be merciful unto us, and bless us.

8th   "   Unto thee lift I up mine eyes, O thou that dwellest in the heavens.

9th   "   Holy, holy, holy, Lord God Almighty!

10th   "   A new commandment I give unto you, that ye love one another.

11th   "   Ask, and it shall be given you.

12th   "   Ye that fear the Lord, bless the Lord.

13th   "   Lord, I believe: help thou mine unbelief.

14th   "   Unto thee, O Lord, do we give thanks.

15th   "   Thine is the kingdom and the power and the glory.

16th   "   Give us this day our daily bread.

17*th Sunday*. Blessed are they that do hunger and thirst **after** righteousness.

18*th*   "   Righteousness and peace have kissed each other.

19*th*   "   Offer the sacrifices of righteousness, and put your trust in the Lord.

20*th*   "   Let not your heart be troubled.

21*st*   "   Teach me, O Lord, the way of thy statutes.

22*d*   "   Stand in awe and sin not.

23*d*   "   No servant can serve two masters.

24*th*   "   Many are the afflictions of the righteous: but the Lord. delivereth him out of them all.

25*th*   "   All my springs are in thee.

26*th*   "   Thy statutes have been my song in the house of my pilgrimage.

27*th*   "   Peace be within thy walls, O Jerusalem.

28*th*   "   Jesus said, Suffer little children to come unto me.

29*th*   "   Mine eyes are ever toward the Lord.

30*th*   "   Lord, I have loved the habitation of thine house.

31*st*   "   Holiness becometh thine house, O Lord, forever.

32*d*   "   Forever, O Lord, thy Word is settled in heaven.

33*d*   "   How lovely are thy tabernacles, O Lord of hosts.

34*th*   "   He shall give his angels charge over thee.

35*th*   "   Thine eyes shall see Jerusalem a holy habitation.

36*th*   "   Ho! every one that thirsteth, come ye to the waters.

37*th*   "   Wherewith shall a young man cleanse his way: by taking heed thereto according to thy Word.

38*th*   "   With my whole heart have I sought thee: O, let me not wander from thy commandments.

39*th*   "   Come unto me, all ye that labor and are heavy laden, and I will give you rest.

40*th* *Sunday.* Rest in the Lord, and wait patiently for him.

41*st* " He that keepeth thee will not slumber.

42*d* " So teach us to number our days that we may apply our hearts unto wisdom.

43*d* " Wait on the Lord, be of good courage, and he shall strengthen thine heart.

44*th* " Honor thy father and thy mother.

45*th* " Make me to go in the path of thy commandments.

46*th* " Create in me a clean heart, O God.

47*th* " Gracious is the Lord and righteous.

48*th* " Return unto thy rest, O my soul, for the Lord hath dealt bountifully with thee.

49*th* " The Lord reigneth: let the earth rejoice.

50*th* " Remember, O Lord, thy tender mercies and thy loving-kindnesses; for they have been even of old.

51*st* " O, send out thy light and thy truth, let them lead me: let them bring me unto thy holy hill and to thy tabernacles.

52*d* " The Lord shall keep thy going out and thy coming in, from this time forth and for evermore.

NOTE.—The intelligent teacher will be able to use each of these texts as the topic of a simple and practical religious lesson for the class on the Sunday when it is recited.

THE TEN BLESSINGS.

MATT. V: 3–12.

Blessed are the poor in spirit; for theirs is the kingdom of heaven.

Blessed are they that mourn; for they shall be comforted.

Blessed are the meek; for they shall inherit the earth.

Blessed are they which do hunger and thirst after righteousness; for they shall be filled.

Blessed are the merciful; for they shall obtain mercy.

Blessed are the pure in heart; for they shall see God.

Blessed are the peace-makers; for they shall be called the children of God.

Blessed are they which are persecuted for righteousness' sake; for theirs is the kingdom of heaven.

Blessed are ye, when men shall revile you and persecute you, and shall say all manner of evil against you falsely, for my sake.

Rejoice and be exceeding glad; for great is your reward in heaven.

THE GOLDEN RULE.

ALL things whatsoever ye would that men should do unto you, do ye even so to them; for this is the law and the prophets.—Matt. vii: 12.

INDEX

TO THE HYMNS, SONGS, AND CHANTS.

Lightning Source UK Ltd.
Milton Keynes UK
UKHW010608120219
337137UK00007B/1499/P